# BEHAVIOUR

BEHAVIOUR

# Behaviour

D. E. BROADBENT

UNIVERSITY PAPERBACKS

METHUEN : LONDON

*First published 1961 by Eyre & Spottiswoode (Publishers) Ltd*
*First published in this series 1964*
*Reprinted twice*
*Reprinted 1968*
*S.B.N. 416 68490 4*
*1.4*
*Printed and bound in Great Britain by*
*Butler & Tanner Ltd, Frome and London*

*University Paperbacks are published by*
METHUEN & CO LTD
*11 New Fetter Lane London EC4*

'Melancholy folk, for instance, from physical causes are often unnecessarily timid. Therefore, since this is the case, since bodily disposition affects the passions in this way, it is clear that such affections are forms existing in matter, that is to say, they exist in a corporeal way. And for this reason their boundaries, that is, the definition of these dispositions, must not be constructed without including matter; so that if anger were to be defined, it would be described as a motion of a certain body, say, the heart, or of some part or faculty of such a body. . . . If therefore such attributes do not belong to the soul alone, but to the body also, it follows necessarily that matter enters into their definition; but everything into which corporeal substance or matter enters, is in the province of the natural philosopher; therefore attributes of this nature are to be studied by the natural philosopher. But further it is his task, whose function it is to consider the attributes, to consider their subject as well. And hence it is the duty of the physicist to study the soul.'

St Thomas Aquinas. Commentary on Aristotle's 'De Anima'

'We are made and yet are more than what made us.'

Arthur Miller. Introduction to the Collected Plays

# Foreword

It is a cliché nowadays to say that our mastery of the material world is outstripping our ability to control ourselves. Men send rockets out to the stars, release the sources of energy used by the Sun itself, and recombine the fundamental particles of matter to make new kinds of clothing: but they still steal, go mad, live unhappily together, and threaten each other with weapons which might destroy the entire species. It is urgent that our behaviour should be brought up to the standard of our knowledge, and there is therefore no lack of voices urging possible remedies in the form of creeds, political systems, economic policies, and so on.

But perhaps the most hopeful road is to apply to behaviour itself the method of attack which has proved so useful in dealing with the material world: to observe, experiment, and build predictive theories for further experimental test. This road is being tried with vigour and enthusiasm by a band of men who are small in numbers compared with those in older sciences, and who are much less widely known. To some extent their activities are linked with those in other fields. As physicists and engineers prepare to launch satellites into space, these students of behaviour are trying out on the ground the controls which eventually men will have to use beyond the atmosphere. These trials ensure that the controls are easy to handle and that no confusion or fumbling is likely to occur. As the chemists produce a new drug, it is given to animals and the effects on behaviour studied carefully. As computing machines become more widely available, they are applied to the analysis of the thousands of actions which a man may produce in half an hour; and the organization of the nervous system is compared with that of the computers themselves.

Traditional views of human nature would find it strange that any analogy should exist between men and machines. Our feelings rightly revolt at the implication that human activity is no more meaningful than that of a clockwork toy. Nevertheless at a simple level there is a legitimate resemblance between the way our limbs are put together, on the one hand, and the functioning of mechanical systems of levers on the other. Such a comparison helps us to understand our bodies. At a more complex level, many modern machines are concerned not with leverage and energy, but rather with the handling of information. They will translate from one language to another, perform mathematical and logical operations, or try a series of actions before 'learning' to use the most successful. Their behaviour in these tasks obeys more or less simple rules. If now we study the behaviour of an organism in the same way, we can hope to find the exact extent to which it obeys these same rules, and at what point it deviates from them. Such a study ought to sharpen our awareness of the similarities and differences between our own brains and the machines we have made to help them.

In the end this approach is bound to cause an upheaval in our ideas about human personality. The frame of reference in which most civilized thought proceeds is one which distinguishes sharply between an impersonal world and an internal, acutely personal, one. The concepts employed within the latter – wishes, anxieties, memories – are altogether different in kind from those used to describe the physical world. This distinction appears not only in everyday speech, but also in those forms of psychology which are most widely known. It exists in philosophical discussions of the nature of knowledge, and it exists in the psycho-analytic accounts of human nature which are so widely used by doctors in the treatment of neurosis. The work of Freud especially has provided a systematic description of the ways in which desires and fears may interact beneath the surface of conventional life. Such a description is a response to the immediate need of patients in trouble; and has brought peace of mind to many people, with the conviction that they have achieved understanding of themselves. Yet because the concepts used by psycho-analysts are derived from experience, they need to be accepted through an experienced certainty of their truth. They cannot readily be linked to the kind of observations made in the rest of medicine: and it is uncommonly difficult to resolve disagreements which may arise between psycho-analysts whose experiences happen to be different. For these reasons, and quite regardless of the value of the Freudian point of view, it is worth while also to develop the analysis of behaviour in terms which refer to the public world rather than to the inner one.

While therefore most modern thought has continued to divide human beings sharply from the natural phenomena around them, an attack upon this division has been quietly growing in strength. As yet it is largely unknown to most people: but it is beginning to raise questions which are profoundly disturbing to almost all of us. What ought our attitude to be to our own actions, if they can be even partially understood through mechanical analogies? Ought we to despise ourselves for it? Or, if there is a continuity between personality and nature, ought we to regard the outside world in a less impersonal fashion than has been customary in recent years? The advance of this branch of science threatens to make an impact upon our philosophies which will be at least as great as the impact of Darwinism. But our complex society cannot afford the time which was taken to assimilate the implications of Darwinism: it only needs a wave of fanaticism or of contempt for humanity, and we shall all be dead. The spread of such knowledge as we do have about behaviour is a matter of urgency; and above all more effort is needed to increase that knowledge. The purpose of the following pages is therefore to summarize the achievements of the behaviourist approach up to the present day, and to try to communicate a sense of the immensely significant problems which are beginning to appear at the edge of our researches, like whales stranded by a receding tide of ignorance. The tide goes out slowly, its motion being invisible while it is watched: but the implications of that motion are all-important to men. As the possibilities of experimental psychology grow more and more evident, the subject becomes of concern not merely to a few specialists but to everybody. This book therefore is not a work of scholarship. It concentrates upon the positive progress which is being made in the study of behaviour, rather than upon the points of weakness which are still numerous in our present views. The elimination of these weaknesses, and the advancement of the borders of knowledge, are of gripping interest to most professional psychologists. In our learned writings therefore we rightly emphasize points on which existing opinion should be changed. But this is not the place for such advances: it is a place instead to set down on paper the fascination of probing the most baffling problems that have ever faced science. That fascination may catch hold of some who read, and bring them to interrogate Nature on this subject for themselves. If so, the extra reinforcements will be of value to the little band of devoted enquirers; and some excuse may be found for the applied psychologist who left his proper concerns to write this book.

Thanks are due to the Cresset Press for permission to reproduce the quotation from Arthur Miller's Introduction to his *Collected Plays*: and to Messrs J. M. Dent for permission to quote from the Everyman edition of Father M. C. D'Arcy's *Selected Writings of St Thomas Aquinas*.

DONALD BROADBENT

Applied Psychology Unit of the Medical Research Council
 Cambridge
 1960

# Contents

# I

# Why Behaviour?

In the far-off days before the First World War, a man named J. B. Watson coined the word 'behaviourism', and under that title stated an attitude to psychology which aroused great enthusiasm in some people: and equally great antagonism in others. As a result, his name is probably as well known to laymen as that of his contemporary Lord Rutherford, the nuclear physicist. But whereas the layman usually has some idea of the trend of nuclear physics since Edwardian times, he has little knowledge of Watson's successors in psychology. The reason is presumably that neither psychology in general nor behaviourism in particular is likely to blow the layman's body to the four winds: nor will they light and heat his home after the world's stocks of oil are gone. The practical effects of nuclear physics, whether good or evil, are more spectacular than those of the study of behaviour. This may not be true in the future. Even in 1960 experimental psychology has a number of useful applications: but as yet nuclear physics is more useful, and therefore attracts attention even from the most determinedly unscientific of humanists.

Yet practical consequences are not everything. The same humanist, whose familiarity with Oppenheimer's role in the development of the H-bomb is balanced by his ignorance of Skinner's role in the analysis of operant conditioning, is often the man who professes contempt for mere technology. Science, he may say, is concerned only with the inferior material circumstances of life. Far more important are the problems of personal adjustment and of the nature of man. At this point in the argument there is usually a concealed assumption that the study of history or literature sheds more light on these spiritual problems than science does. This assumption tends to be unconvincing to scientists: but many of them would agree with the early stages of the argument. If physics can shed any light on philosophy, that contribution is as real as nuclear power. We want to understand the world as well as manipulating it. If physics can contribute in this way, surely the study of behaviour can do so even more? When we look at inorganic matter, any inferences to our own nature must be indirect: the facts most relevant to ourselves come from sources closer to ourselves. Even though Watson's successors may have made no bombs, their provision of facts about living creatures gives them a claim on the attention of all of us.

We must not, of course, expect too much. Perfect knowledge of all the laws of nature (assuming such knowledge to be possible or even meaningful) would probably still be consistent with numerous different attitudes to life. Our own knowledge is very imperfect, even in physics, and the implications to be drawn from it are correspondingly more open to argument. The tentative conclusions of behaviourists since Watson's time will not therefore turn the entrance of the Church of England into a one-way street: but they deserve, in any assessment of the world, at least as much weight as do the properties of electrons. The following pages, therefore, try to tell the story of behaviourism over the past fifty years, in broad and simplified outline. We shall see that many of Watson's original views have been forced out of scientific circulation by the pressure of experiment. Some of his other ideas have spread until almost all psychologists accept them. So as a beginning to our story we ought to look at his views and try to understand how he came to put them forward.

## Classical Introspectionism: Examining One's Thoughts

Any short description of psychology as it was at the beginning of the twentieth century must be a caricature. The main feature of the subject was that different eminent men held rather different views, so that one would have to go into a lot of detail to cover all of them. It is perhaps fair to say, though, that the majority thought the main purpose of psychology to be the study of human experience. What was the content of man's consciousness in various situations, and what were the processes within it? A great deal of effort was put into finding answers to these questions, using more or less rigorous methods. People were placed repeatedly in controlled situations, such as looking at particular lights or listening to certain sounds. They were asked to observe their own experience and to report exactly what it was. This meant a rather sophisticated form of observation, and usually the people used were trained in this type of process. In principle, though, the technique could be justified in the same way as techniques of observation in the physical sciences. If we want to carry out an accurate measurement of length, we choose an observer who is careful and attentive to making his readings: so also when we want to know something about the nature of experience we should choose a careful observer. It could even be argued that the nature of the observation is really the same in both cases. No observer can do more than report his experience; in physics we make use of experiences such as seeing a pointer indicate a particular reading. In psychology our interest is in the experience itself rather than in the pointer-reading, but the principle might be held to be the same. The main difference was that in psychology one must take great care to report the content of consciousness and not inferences about the events in the outer world which give rise to that content. One must not say 'I see a pointer which reads such-and-such' but report the actual pattern and colour of one's visual awareness. Some books on philosophy take rather this approach even today, asserting that one is sure of sensations such as colour and form, and that knowledge of the external world is inferred from these sensory data. The aim of the introspective psychologists was to make a list of the basic data and an account of the processes of inference.

17

Broadly speaking, this type of observation found three kinds of element in consciousness. There were *sensations*, which were experiences stemming directly from stimulation of the sense-organs, the eye, the ear, and so on. There were *images*, which resembled sensations but arose within the mind itself without any stimulation of the senses. There were also *feelings*, which could be described by such adjectives as pleasant or unpleasant, and provided the emotional tone of experience. By Watson's time, however, this division was running into certain difficulties. In spite of the care taken to secure accurate observation, different laboratories found different results in their introspections. Let us take three examples.

If you suddenly look up and see a man-eating tiger, you will probably say that you feel fear. You will also suffer certain bodily changes, of a kind which are useful if you run away or engage the tiger in unarmed combat. You will receive sensations from these bodily changes just as you do from your eyes and ears: your stomach will probably feel queasy, and you may notice your heart pounding. Now the suggestion was made by James and by Lange that the emotion of fear is purely the set of sensations arising from the bodily changes. This suggestion was sharply criticized, because some people hold that when one is afraid, there is something in consciousness as well as these sensations. Other people support the James-Lange theory: and it is probably fair to suspect the existence of a third group who get more and more confused the more they think about the question. Introspection did not seem able to solve this problem.

Another difficulty arose from the question of mixed feelings. When a rose is presented to your nostrils, you may report particular sensations of smell, and perhaps some experience of cold from the air drawn into your nose, and of strain in the chest-muscles used in sniffing. Along with these sensations there will most likely be a feeling of pleasure, which you can distinguish from the sensations themselves.

On the other hand, if you hear the squeak of chalk on a blackboard, the background feeling may be one of unpleasantness. Now suppose some enquiring psychologist presents both a rose and a chalk-squeak simultaneously. The sensations may well be simply those met previously, but all arriving together and so with an altered degree of clarity. What about the feelings? Does one have pleasant and unpleasant feelings at the same time, or do the two cancel out, or do they alternate rapidly? You might perhaps describe your experience as one of pleasantness at the focus of attention with a surrounding background of unpleasantness: and there are a very large number of other possibilities. Once again, different laboratories come to rather different conclusions on the subject of mixed feelings.

But the most celebrated controversy of this sort was that about 'imageless thought'. A group of investigators working at Würzburg claimed that some of the most important elements of thought could not be reported in terms of sensations or images. One might have the 'bare awareness' of a concept without even the most generalized mental picture embodying it. Possibly even more important, one might establish a 'determining tendency' which would decide the line that thought should follow but wouldn't provide any clear, reportable, conscious content. As this is rather a difficult notion, perhaps we should consider an example. Suppose you say to someone, 'I am going to give you a number. When you hear it, add two to it and give me the answer.' Most people agree that after such a question the listener will have quite a lot going on in his mind. He may conjure up shapes which he associates with various numbers, he may hear echoes of your words, he may have feelings of nervousness and tenseness. All this confusion then settles down, according to the Würzburgers, to a fairly calm state of readiness in which there are no pictures or relevant sensations to be reported. When you say 'six' the answer 'eight' comes straight into the listener's awareness without any-thing intervening that he can tell you about. Yet for the answer to be correct there must have been something important in his mind before it appeared – and he could not introspect this vital something. A particularly clear instance is provided by a rather flamboyant experiment in which the subject is hypnotized, given the instruction 'add', and then returned to normal consciousness and asked for the first number to come into his head on being shown, say, three and five. He says 'eight', but cannot tell from inspecting his own experience why he does so.

The possibility of imageless thought was keenly attacked by other introspectionists. There was always, they said, some conscious content for a really good observer to report. It might not look relevant to the topic of thought, it might simply consist of sensations of pressure in certain parts of the body or an image so unlike a real object that a good deal of literary ability was required to describe it. But a complete vacuum would never occur in the mind.

Imageless thought, then (along with mixed feelings and the existence of emotional feelings apart from bodily sensations), was a topic on which people could not agree just by examining their own experience. If we want to understand the effect which such controversies had upon Watson, it is worth emphasizing the difference between these disagreements and those in other sciences. Of course, physicists and physiologists disagree with one another, often acrimoniously, and with all the vices of obscurantism, self-interest, and authority-worship shown in human quarrels in nonscientific fields. If all psychologists thought alike it would mean that the subject was dead. But the trouble with these arguments between introspectionists was that they were not about methods of experiment or the interpretation of results, but seemed to be about the results of experiments. There is no real harm in the difference of approach between radio-astronomers and those who use optical telescopes: nor anything discreditable in the absence of agreement concerning the theory of continuous creation. But if one astronomer said that he could see Mars in one part of the sky and another that he could see it somewhere else, the controversy would obviously be very discreditable to somebody. If it went on for more than a very short time, it would be discreditable to the subject as a whole. It was in this light that many psychologists saw the disagreement between different introspectionists. They became impatient with the elaborate analysis of experience which had led to such doubtful conclusions, and were ready to join a movement which rejected it. Watson's was the movement which resulted.

Later on in this chapter we shall look at the value of introspection more closely. For the moment it is enough to point out that these controversies were not purely about facts. The 'determining tendency' was not only an item in consciousness: even when it could not be reported at all it was advanced as a reason for the appearance of other items. In other words, the Würzburgers wanted causes and explanations for the emergence of certain images and feelings rather than others. Consciousness itself could not provide these causes; one cannot adequately explain by introspection why a particular number is accompanied by a visual image of, say, a half-moon, nor what it is that causes the correct answer to rise into consciousness, when one hears the question 'Add five and three'. Psychiatrists have been known, when faced with some peculiarly distressing conscious phenomenon such as a prostrating dread of running water, to find a traumatic episode in the patient's past life which seems to most people a reasonable explanation of the dread. Yet this explanation was quite unknown to the patient. Such exploits were beginning to become popular in the years just before behaviourism began: Freud's *Interpretation of Dreams* was published in 1900, and by 1909 he was sufficiently famous to be invited to an academic ceremony at Clark University in America. There was in fact a growing feeling that the facts of consciousness were not enough, and the 'determining tendency' was a symptom of that feeling. In America especially there was a school (known as functionalists) who treated the data of conscious experience against the background of evolution. The explanation for the strange loops and associations in the thought of each individual lies in the process of adjustment going on between him and his surroundings. So one needs to know facts about him other than his conscious processes, and to try and see the causal connections between these material facts and his awareness.

So far we have seen two forces at work in Edwardian psychology: the revulsion created by disagreement about the facts of consciousness, and the pressure to merge those facts in a larger biological background. There was a third force, which arose from the fact that by the 1900's many psychologists were studying animals rather than men. They did so for obvious reasons; one of the standard techniques of science is to study simpler systems as a guide to more complex ones, and so one might legitimately hope to see more clearly in animals principles which in man are hidden by the enormous variety of his experience. In addition, one cannot for moral reasons control the surroundings, heredity, and upbringing of a child as one can those of an animal. One can even carry out operations on the nervous system of animals and study the effects, which is obviously impossible in man except when the brain is already injured. But when animals are being observed, there is no direct method of studying their consciousness. We can only see how they behave. The technique used, in the days when Watson was trained, was to infer that the animal had the experience which a man would have if he behaved in the same way. Watson himself wrote a monograph in 1907 on the bodily sensations of a rat learning to find its way through a maze. But to say the least, this is a very doubtful procedure. It was modified by the rule known as Lloyd Morgan's Canon, that one should never assume the animal to have a higher 'psychical faculty' than the simplest possible to explain its behaviour. Yet how can a creature of one species possibly be sure of the experience of a member of a quite different species? Would it not be safer simply to state the behaviour of the animal under various conditions, and go no further? And if this was done, how should one compare knowledge gained from animals with that acquired from the study of human beings? Here was the third force tending to make psychologists dissatisfied with their existing methods. Introspection gave conflicting results, it did not provide the explanations for its own data, and it made comparison with animals difficult. It was not surprising that when in 1913 Watson published a paper putting forward a new creed, the idea was seized on eagerly and a complete movement leaped into being. Watson did not provide a set of strange but systematic concepts which his academic colleagues gradually thought over and found good. Rather he expressed simply and vigorously a number of unformulated attitudes which already existed, and so provided a rallying-point for many of the more productive psychologists of his time. In fact he resigned from his academic job in 1920, only seven years after his celebrated paper, and yet behaviourism continued as a large and flourishing movement. It could hardly have done so if it had rested on his contribution alone. But he was the representative and the protagonist, and it is his views (or a distorted version of them) which are usually meant when the word behaviourism is casually used in modern writings.

## Watson's Creed

As has already been implied, the first statements of behaviourism consisted of a number of assertions which were only loosely connected with one another, so that later generations can accept some and reject others. They were also largely assertions of attitude or method of procedure rather than factual propositions, so that argument about them is on a rather philosophical level. Facts were to come later, and we shall reach them in the following chapters. For the rest of this one we shall continue to be somewhat abstract, with apologies to those who are impatient of philosophizing. Such impatience is very understandable, but there is no point in giving the results of a method before the method itself is accepted: and to some people facts about behaviour may seem irrelevant to psychology if they are served up without justification.

Watson himself was clearly a person impatient of refined verbal distinctions and anxious to get on with the job. As a result his views have been anathema to many philosophers who were over-aware of the weaknesses in his wording. Three points stand out in his teaching: the rejection of introspection in principle, the belief that environment rather than heredity determines human behaviour, and the assertion that this effect of environment is chiefly through a particular process of conditioning reflexes which we shall explain in a moment.

His *rejection of introspection* solved at one blow the difficulties mentioned in the last section. Once this unsatisfactory source of data had gone there should be no more disagreement over facts, no problem of finding causes for the occurrence of this thought rather than that, and the facts of human psychology would be of the same kind as those of animal workers. Just as the rat is observed to turn into one alley of a maze rather than another, so one can study the movements of human beings and compare the results of experiments on them with those on other species. In neither case is there any need to drag in conscious experience. This attitude has sometimes been regarded as a denial of the reality of consciousness, but it is hard to find any statement by Watson which goes so far. All he said was that science, being a public process, must ignore private awareness and deal only with those data which are available to everyone. Such a distinction between subjective and objective seems reasonable enough, although of course it remained open for anybody to value the subjective more highly: and it is likely that much of the antagonism which Watson aroused was rooted in the feeling that subjective aspects of human nature are so overwhelmingly important that no objective study at all can be appropriate. We shall return to this point when we consider how far Watson's views have survived.

An objection of a rather different sort is that human beings are clearly much more complex than any other animal, so that such observations as 'time taken to solve problems' or 'number of alleys entered in a maze' would not give adequate information for understanding human behaviour. People spend much time sitting and thinking, rather than rushing about: what objective measures can be applied in such cases? To this Watson replied that thinking might be a process very similar to speech, but with the size of the movements so reduced that they could no longer be seen or heard. In principle such movements might be detected by very sensitive recording equipment, and so allow objective recording of thought. He also suggested that measurement of bodily change, particularly in the sexual organs, could substitute for the 'feeling' of the introspectionist. It will be noticed that these are suggestions about questions of fact, and so are rather different from the rejection of conscious experience, which was a rule of procedure. As facts these suggestions have been only partially successful. Certainly the muscles used in speech are active in thought, at least in some people: since Watson's time it has become possible to detect this activity electrically. But it has not yet been shown that the muscles move in a different way for one thought rather than another, and this is essential if they are to provide us with an improvement on introspection. In the same way bodily changes do undoubtedly occur in emotion, as was known well before Watson. But no pattern of bodily changes has yet been shown to characterize any particular emotion: people turn white with rage and also with fear, that is, the blood vessels in their skin contract and so force the blood to the muscles to provide fuel for violent action. In both those emotions, and in others too, sweating may occur and so assist the body to keep its temperature constant even though the muscles are generating heat. But one cannot (at least as yet) look at the records of the bodily changes and say which of the possible emotions the man has experienced. It is still open for future research to show subtle differences of pattern, both in emotional response and in the activity of the speech muscles during thought, but neither is yet established. To Watson, however, these possibilities offered a way of escape from the criticism that measuring behaviour alone excludes many important processes from psychology.

*His extreme belief in environment* was also a guess about facts rather than a rule of procedure. He carried it to a point where heredity was allowed scarcely any weight in determining behaviour. Yet there was certainly insufficient evidence for such a sweeping conclusion: even now our knowledge is not clear-cut about the role of heredity in behaviour. It is therefore worth remembering two factors which would make the influence of environment more important in Watson's eyes. Firstly, the tradition of orthodox psychology lay rather in that direction. If one asked why a man reported a visual image of a blue sky on hearing the word 'California', the answer given by classical psychologists would often be that the idea of a blue sky had been 'associated' with that of California through the frequent occurrence of the two in close succession. Knowledge of the outside world could, according to the dominant stream of philosophical psychology, come only through the senses; and so most of the furniture of mental life could only be acquired by learning. When behaviour replaced conscious experience as the main interest of psychologists, there was a carry-over of the explanations formerly used. Since learning had been the explanation given for many introspective reports, it continued to be used to explain behaviour.

But in addition there was a second factor increasing the interest of early behaviourists in learning. Any explanations of an animal's (or man's) actions in terms of his past environment have the great advantage of being entirely in terms of events we can observe. When we say that a rat turns into an alley because it was fed in that alley, we are speaking only of publicly ascertainable facts. If the tendency to turn into the alley was somehow built into the animal by heredity, we would want to know the way it was built in: and this cannot be found out by observing the animal's actions. So there was and is a good deal of pressure to explain as much as possible as the result of environmental influence.

Watson's emphasis on learning thus came as a natural consequence of his rejection of introspection, but there is of course no necessary connection between the two. One can believe in the importance of heredity without rejecting objective experimental methods: in fact, most geneticists would be very surprised to find their subject regarded as less scientific than the learning experiments of psychologists. None the less Watson himself thought that the only inherited features of behaviour were simple reflexes such as the series of movements performed in swallowing something put in the mouth. All more complex actions were to him habits resulting from learning.

His emphasis on *conditioned reflexes* first became public in 1916, when he gave a presidential address to the American Psychological Association. In it he appealed to the work of Pavlov on conditioned reflexes as showing the units from which these habits were constructed. Pavlov's experiments were then novel, although they have since become as familiar as Watson's own name: for he launched them to a dominant position in psychology by this 1916 address and the books which followed it. In a simplified form the central facts of conditioning are these. When a dog sees food, its mouth waters. If a bell is rang on a number of occasions shortly before the food is seen, then the saliva will flow when the bell is presented even though no food is given. The action which was once a response to food is now a response to the bell.

This experiment was interpreted by Watson, and by most people at the time, in a way which is now rather unpopular. Mention has already been made of reflex actions, which Watson agreed to be hereditary. They are very simple responses which normally appear quite predictably when a certain stimulus is applied. As most of us know, a tap to the tendon just below and in front of the knee will cause the leg to extend and make a kicking movement without any conscious voluntary decision. Another example is the contraction of the pupil of the eye when a bright light is shone upon it. Now the conditioning experiments were thought of as showing that the motor part of a reflex, the action, could be transferred to another stimulus simply through this stimulus being present just before the action was carried out: nothing else being necessary to produce the change. This conception of 'stimulus-response association by contiguity' is really very similar to the old-fashioned 'association of ideas' which we mentioned earlier. Introspective psychology explained that the word 'California' produced a visual image of a blue sky because the word and the sensation had often occurred together: so behaviourism now said that an action occurred in a certain situation because that action had often occurred in the same situation previously. On both theories it is merely contiguity in time which is necessary for an association to be found.

But to Watson this view of conditioning was particularly useful, because with it he could claim to have an explanation in principle of all the complex behaviour of adult animals and men: and he need not appeal to unobservable faculties within the mind. On his view the child was born with a few simple reflexes, and then transferred these responses to fresh stimuli, recombined and refined them by the mechanism of conditioning, and so developed his own individual repertoire of behaviour. For instance, a child might show a number of responses which the onlooker would call 'showing fear' when a loud noise was suddenly made. If this noise happened to occur whenever a woolly animal was in sight, that animal would produce the 'fear' responses. Watson actually carried out an experiment of this type to verify the deduction from animal research to child development, and got the results he expected. This, of course, did not necessarily mean that his theory was correct in other ways.

## The Verdict of Posterity

When we try to assess how much of Watson's creed can still be held, it is useful to take his three main beliefs in the opposite order to that used in the last section. This is because the belief in behaviour rather than consciousness is much more fundamental than the other doctrines. As we saw, it is easy to understand how a man who wanted to stick to observable evidence might incline towards emphasizing the environment, and also appeal to conditioning as the mechanism of learning. So we should really clear these secondary beliefs out of the way, and then discuss the main point in rather more detail.

Firstly, there is no doubt that Watson's trust in learning by contiguity was misplaced. The facts of conditioning experiments are indeed as they were given in the last section, and as Watson believed them: but there are many other facts which soon became impossible to ignore, and which did not fit in with Watson's simple idea of switching responses from one stimulus to another. The central difficulty was that the response which is finally learned is not necessarily the one which has happened most often in the situation. The animal (or man) may make a 'wrong' response many times before abandoning it and turning to the 'correct' one. For instance, a rat in a maze may turn to the left on first seeing a particular junction, and do so over and over again. On the simple Watsonian theory, turning left should thus be firmly established as the response to seeing this part of the maze. But if the left turn leads to a cul-de-sac, and the right turn to a box of food, the rat will eventually stop turning left and learn to turn right. It is quite difficult to make a rat or a dog behave in a manner which we would not regard as sensible; whereas if any response could be shifted to a new stimulus merely by appearing in the neighbourhood of that stimulus it should be easy to make an animal look foolish.

There are other difficulties, which are connected with this main one. Successful conditioning needs a hungry animal, although hunger was not a central factor in Watson's theory: and even when conditioning has been achieved the dog does not respond to the bell in the same way that it does to the sight of food. Some parts of its behaviour, such as the mouth watering, may be similar but others, such as muscular movements, are quite different. Furthermore, if a response is produced again and again by its conditioned stimulus without ever being called forth by its natural one, it disappears: if we ring the bell again and again without ever giving the dog food, its mouth stops watering. Yet a man's behaviour may continue to be the same over long periods without any presentation of stimuli other than those to which he has learned to react. If he is frightened of woolly animals, he goes on being frightened of them even although nobody fires a revolver behind him every time he sees a panda.

These experimental results, and others like them, have made it impossible to accept Watson's view of conditioning in its original simplicity. This verdict emphatically does not mean that conditioning experiments are irrelevant to the explanation of behaviour; it is merely directed at the particular theory of conditioning which supposes that the more often an animal does something in a particular situation, the more often it will do so in the future. In the next chapter we shall look at the modern view of learning, and will see that some people (particularly Guthrie) have theories which are not so very different from Watson's. Yet there is no doubt that his account of the mechanism of learning left out very important points.

What about his general emphasis on learning? Here we must be slightly more cautious in our criticism, for it is probably true that psychologists place more emphasis on environment now than they ever did previously. Some of this emphasis is doubtless a matter of fashion, since evidence is very hard to obtain. For example, most newspaper readers are now familiar with the view that delinquency or mental illness may be traced back to deprivation of mother-love in childhood. Much (not all) of the evidence for this view comes from records showing a higher proportion of unsatisfactory homes in the background of delinquents and patients than in that of normal people. But it is of course quite likely that a parent who is unresponsive to social pressure, and so abandons a child or treats it harshly, may tend to pass on by heredity this lack of social sensitivity. If bad parents have bad children, that is no evidence against heredity. It is only fair to add that the common belief that ability must be inherited, because of the number of eminent men found in certain families, is equally fallacious. Great men naturally provide a highly stimulating environment for their relatives, and so might well give rise to greater ability amongst them even though heredity played no part in behaviour. If nature and nurture are both left uncontrolled to play whatever part they can, we can draw no conclusions.

Ideally, we would have to find people with different environments but the same heredity or vice versa, if we wanted to get a perfect measurement of the importance of either factor. This is impossible, but there are methods of research which come fairly close to the ideal. For instance, we can look at children in orphanages and similar institutions, and test their ability. The surroundings of the children in one institution are very much the same for all: differences between them might indeed be due to chance, causing one child to receive more of a teacher's attention than another, but the intelligence of the lost parents should not affect the ability of an orphanage child unless heredity is of some importance. One snag in the research is that since the parents are lost we cannot measure their performance on our tests. But we can find out the kind of work they did and in England people in some jobs tend to be more intelligent than those in others. There is some evidence that children brought up in institutions tend to have the ability which one expects for the job of their lost parent. So this ability must to some extent be inherited.

From the opposite point of view, one can look at the abilities of identical twins. Such twins have, we believe, the same heredity and are sometimes separated in very early life so that they may have environments different to some degree. When this is done their abilities may turn out rather different, sufficiently for one twin to pass a school selection procedure which the other twin would have failed. So environment must affect ability. On the other hand, the largest differences recorded between twins brought up apart are still much smaller than the range of ability in the population as a whole: so these results also show that heredity plays some part together with environment.

If this is so, why did we say earlier that psychologists now place more emphasis than ever before on the environment? Just as the evidence now forbids us to rule out heredity as completely as Watson did, so also there is evidence which forbids us to rule out the environment. The results already mentioned were found in Britain, and the U.S.A., and this fact places limits upon the number of different environments which were involved. Homes, schools, and other influences upon people living in the United Kingdom may seem to us to vary a good deal: but they have more in common with each other than they do with homes and education in distant parts of the world. Since Watson's time information about societies other than our familiar European one has become more plentiful, and perhaps taken more into account. It has become obvious that much of the behaviour taken for granted by each society as natural and inborn cannot really be so, but must be instilled by the 'culture pattern' of the society itself. If we hear of a primitive tribe who regard all men as naturally co-operative, considerate, and peaceful, we might be tempted to suppose that their heredity differs from our own. But when we find other tribes in the same area who seem to belong to the same physical race and yet show an almost Victorian belief in competition, aggressiveness and the rights of the strong, it becomes difficult to blame these differences in personality upon heredity. Even such apparently deep-rooted traits as the behaviour regarded as typical of male and female have been shown to differ radically in different groups of the same bodily make-up. Some anthropologists have been so impressed by the richness and diversity of the differences in behaviour between different societies that they have used almost Watsonian language about the power of the social group to mould individual behaviour. This is going too far: for the reasons already given, we know that innate endowment plays a part. Indeed in the reports of the anthropologists one sometimes finds mention of the deviant person who cannot fit in to the group into which he was born. In addition, to anticipate the next chapter, it is doubtful whether any society could teach its members modes of behaviour which leave certain innate drives unsatisfied: for it is through that satisfaction that learning most easily takes place. None the less it is now apparent that very much of a man's behaviour is influenced by the group in which he grows up, that is, by his environment. We do not now believe, as some Victorians did, that societies which lack our material triumphs are peopled by men with inferior heredity, almost half-way to the apes along the evolutionary scale. It is the culture of such 'primitive' societies which causes their manner of thought to differ from our own.

To give specific examples in which numerical measurement has been applied, we may turn to a large country such as the United States, within which there is room for small social groups to develop their own patterns of behaviour uninfluenced by the rest of society. Negroes living in the Southern States, for instance, form such a sub-culture: they go to different schools from their white neighbours, and live a generally separate life. In the Northern States this is less true. Correspondingly, Northern Negroes do better than Southern ones on intelligence tests devised by white Americans. This difference is not due to a migration of the more gifted Negroes to the greater opportunities of the North: for the scores increase with the length of time spent in the North. So the inferior ability of Southern Negroes must be put down to their different environment.*

A rather similar argument can be applied to the case of white Americans living in isolated places such as rural mountain areas. Children from such places do worse in intelligence tests than do children from the regions in more normal contact with the outer world. Once again, this cannot be because families of low hereditary quality chose to live in these remote spots: because the children are relatively more inferior the older they are, that is, the longer they have spent in the poor environment.

The tests on which these results were obtained were naturally not school examinations, which would depend on the quality of the formal teaching given to the child. The tests were as free as they could be made from being tests of material already learned: and as a result of the findings we have mentioned it is now generally agreed that one cannot devise a test which will give a fair comparison of the inherited abilities of two people who come from widely different backgrounds. This attitude allows much more importance to environment than some of Watson's contemporaries would have done. It is for this reason that one can fairly regard modern psychologists as more interested in learning

* The data on which this paragraph is based were obtained over twenty years ago: the discrepancy between North and South Negroes would probably be less now, since their environments are more similar than they used to be.

than their predecessors were. But it must still be remembered that Watson overstated his case. Very wide differences in environment are needed to produce large differences in performance on intelligence tests. The differences in upbringing normally found within the English-speaking countries are not enough to equal the differences produced by heredity, as we can calculate from the experiments on twins and on institutional education. So one certainly cannot write heredity off altogether as a cause of behaviour: if we are only thinking of people from our own society, it is the major cause of the differences in ability which we observe. These findings about human beings are somewhat uncontrolled, since we cannot interfere with the mating or upbringing of people. Animals are a different matter, as we said earlier, and by bringing up under the same conditions the offspring of particularly bright and particularly dull individuals we can show the effect of heredity directly. If we take a group of rats, teach them a maze, select the best learners for breeding, then select the best of their children for remating, and so on, we will obtain a strain of rats which is outstandingly good at learning. This experiment shows how false any rigid antithesis between learning and heredity must ultimately prove, since there are inherited differences in the ability to learn. Watson's emphasis on learning would have been perfectly justified if it had not been taken as excluding heredity. Both factors are closely interwoven and, as we shall see in the next chapter, both form part of a continuous evolutionary process of adjustment between living creatures and their environment.

Watson has therefore been unfortunate in the fate of two of his chief tenets: the unimportance of heredity, and the view that learning was based on a simple transfer of responses from one stimulus to another occurring at the same time. But it will be noticed that the evidence used in rejecting these doctrines was of a kind which Watson would have approved. Measurements of the success or failure of specially selected persons, on tests whose scoring does not depend on the experimenter's subjective judgment, owe nothing to conscious experience. Nor do observations of animal behaviour in conditioning and maze-learning situations. Modern psychologists deny Watson's minor beliefs by using his most central one: for the emphasis on objective methods of experiment, which was a partisan battle-cry in his day, is now a generally accepted doctrine. Some of the reasons for this victory have already been mentioned, and others will appear in the next section when we consider how one can nowadays justify turning away from conscious experience towards behaviour. For the moment we ought to amplify the statement that objective methods are 'generally accepted'. Accepted by whom?

The answer to this question is, primarily, 'those people in the English-speaking countries who engage in pure academic research in psychology'. This immediately excludes large numbers of people who are regarded by the public as authorities on human nature. For example, it excludes many psychiatrists, who are medical men concerned with the treatment of mental illness and rarely possess academic degrees in psychology. Whether university-trained or not, such men find themselves with urgent clinical problems on their hands and must solve them, using any means available. It is therefore usual to find that they rely on intuitive interpretations of their patients' difficulties, more than would be acceptable to academic students of human nature. Naturally one cannot wait for the results of objective experiments on conflict of motives, when one is faced with a patient threatening suicide. Systems of treatment, and of theory, based on experience of the clinical situation have most reasonably been developed: of which the best-known are the various ones stemming from the 'psychoanalytic' views of Freud. These approaches are of value in suggesting experiments, as well as in their immediate practical application: but they cannot all be true, and it is often very difficult to decide exactly what observations would verify or disprove a particular theory. For these reasons they have been viewed with considerable scepticism by psychologists in the ivory towers of the universities. Since the Twenties this scepticism seems to have increased.

The territory captured by objective psychology also excludes much of Europe. A direct approach to conscious experience has remained in more universities there than it has in the Commonwealth or the United States. This is however less of a failure for behaviourism than it appears at first sight, for the numbers of people involved are far less than the corresponding numbers in English-speaking countries. The reason is not hard to imagine: the people who provide money for research jobs are apt to look askance at lines of work which have neither aesthetic value nor undeniable proofs of their validity. An object lesson is provided by the role of psychologists in the German Army during the recent war. They favoured an intuitive approach to the problems of selecting men for higher posts. But unfortunately the intuition of soldiers is likely to disagree with that of psychologists, and in such arguments the latter had no experimental evidence to produce as backing for their claims. In the middle of the war this conflict was resolved by the dismissal of psychologists from the German armed forces. In Britain and America, on the other hand, the exponents of objective method were able to produce facts and figures to support their techniques: for that is the meaning of objective method. It is dangerous to claim the spread of an attitude as evidence for its truth. All the same, the aim of the behaviourist revolution was to substitute evidence for opinion, and so to produce communication between one psychologist and another rather than the sterile clash of subjective judgments. Its worldly success therefore stems from the heart of its approach, just as, on a greater scale, the immense spread of the physical sciences rests on the visible proof they produce of their propositions.

Even within the region we have now marked out as under the sway of techniques which Watson would have approved, there is of course a substantial minority who would resent being called behaviourists. Yet they do not use the methods of systematic introspection which we described earlier, and against which Watson fought. Their experiments are usually much like those of anybody else. Their protest against the trend which surrounds them is rather aimed at the simple mechanical theories so often used to explain behaviour, some of which we shall meet in later chapters. They would prefer to use, as explanations, ideas drawn from the ordinary vocabulary men use to describe their experience; to speak of a certain action as explained by the hope, or repulsion, or imaginative insight of the man who performs it. This attitude has the great virtues of being based in respect for human nature and of showing up the inadequacy of our existing theories. Because of the value which most of us rightly place on the subtleties and beauties of human consciousness, it is likely that the lay reader will lean towards this trust in the language of everyday experience. But despite its attractiveness, and the worthy motives of those who use it, the modern behaviourist believes that its use in serious study of human beings is based on a logical fallacy. At least this is true if no special steps are taken to redefine and purge the words of common speech so that they take on an uncommon meaning. The time has therefore come for us to leave Watson's unsophisticated views, and try to state the fundamental attitude of modern behaviourists.

## The Science of Input and Output

Let us start by agreeing that we wish to accumulate knowledge about animals and human beings, knowledge which will be accepted by all those who have studied the subject. This last clause is a tall order, but at least let us say that we wish to produce the same kind of agreement that other sciences reach in dealing with other aspects of nature. The achievement of this aim will require rather careful selection of the sources of information we use, for some kinds of statement are likely to produce disagreement even when all possible steps have been taken to check on them. For example, the statements about mixed feelings, which were mentioned earlier in the chapter, provoke marked disagreement, and if I say that I can experience mixed feelings nobody can prove or disprove the accuracy of my observation. On the other hand statements about the bodily actions, the behaviour, of men and animals should be verifiable by anybody if they are true. If we compiled a set of laws, each of which said that when certain things are seen or heard by a man he will perform certain actions, these laws could readily be checked. So studies of behaviour can be included in our science of human nature.

Thus far we have followed Watson. But at this point we encounter the valid criticism that too much is being left out of our account of Man. As was said earlier, much of human activity goes on silently within the skull, not in visible action. Unless we take into account a man's experience as well as his behaviour, we sacrifice information even about relatively simple matters. For example, if a man looks directly at a small spot of red or green light in a dark room, he will tell you that he can see it. But if he looks directly at a similar blue spot, he says that he does not see it: although as soon as he glances to one side the spot appears. This means that cells sensitive to blue light are not present in the central part of the eye, which is obviously an important point to know. It may help us to find out the difference between these cells and others, and so come to understand colour vision better. Yet, as the cells do not differ when examined under the microscope, we should not know this fact without admitting the man's experience as evidence.

Watson himself was not so unreasonable as to exclude experiments of this kind, nor need we be. The crucial question to ask is, how do we know that the blue light is invisible? Obviously, because the man tells us so: his mouth and tongue move, producing pressure changes in the air which are meaningful words to us. These words are responses just as much as any other bodily action. We can observe that they regularly occur following presentation of the blue light, and include this fact amongst our laws of behaviour. At first sight this attitude might seem to make all soul-searching and introspection legitimate material for science. In fact this is not so; there are important differences between the example of the blue light and those of mixed feelings or imageless thought. Watson did not make these differences clear, although he seems to have been intuitively aware of them. Others, such as Karl

Lashley, gave more attention to justifying the behaviourist position, and their arguments ran roughly as follows.

When a man sees blue, his experience is intensely real to him, but the essence of it cannot be communicated. All he can do is to say a word which labels that experience, so that he can tell other people whether or not some fresh situation gives him this same quality of awareness. No man can tell whether another is really feeling the same as he does himself when he looks at a colour. Although words do not carry the essence of experience, two different words indicate two experiences different at least to some degree. When a man is faced with a small blue patch and says 'I see nothing', he is telling us that this experience is the same as that he has when no light at all is present. In ordinary laboratory practice it would often be a waste of time to do another experiment to make sure that the man does say 'I see nothing' when we show him nothing – but the value of his introspection depends on the possibility of this other experiment. We only know what he means when he makes remarks about his experience, because we think we know what other situations would provoke the same remarks.

This is not simply a philosophical doctrine without practical consequences. Suppose we want to find how faint a sound can be heard, and therefore we produce sounds of various intensities for somebody to say whether he can hear them or not. Although we can get a rough answer by relying on the everyday meaning of words, we will soon find that doing the experiment over and over again gives rather inconsistent results. To get a really accurate measurement it is necessary to make sure that the listener really does say 'I hear nothing' when nothing is present: to put in occasional catch trials of complete silence without the listener expecting them, and observe what he says. Inexperienced people will often say that they do hear the sound, and have to be taught what they should be listening for. Because of this, all good machines for testing hearing include a silent switch by which the tester can turn off the sound without any indication to the listener. If one is doing an experiment with somebody who has taken part in much previous research, the meaning of his words is fairly well defined by his previous learning, and one can therefore cut down the number of catch trials. But leaving them out altogether, even with experienced subjects, will cause some raised eyebrows among careful experimenters.

It is, then, a necessary precaution in practice to check the exact boundaries between the situations which a man describes in one way and those which he describes in another. We can now see the fatal weakness of the experiments on, for example, mixed feelings. This precaution was not applied, and perhaps is impossible to apply. There was no situation, apart from the appearance of pleasant and unpleasant sensations at the same time, where mixed feelings were expected. Therefore we do not know exactly what the phrase meant to any particular person, and so we cannot tell whether the combatants in the controversy of long ago were really having different experiences or merely calling the same experience by different names. The fallacy, in asking a man to describe the contents of his mind, is that his words cannot convey directly how he feels: they can only list similarities and differences between his state now and his state in other circumstances.

A similar objection applies to the use of concepts such as 'expectancy' or 'insight' to explain actions. It is legitimate to employ such words, provided that we are clear exactly what is meant by them. It is not legitimate simply to use them without explaining them. For example, suppose we see that a trained animal enters a maze, turns right, and reaches food in a box. To say that this is because the animal expects the food, may convey different things to different people. Some might interpret such a statement as implying that the animal has emotional disturbances of the same kind as a man in a similar situation, with perhaps the same changes in the body as a consequence. Others might be doubtful of these interpretations, but would assume that an 'expectant' animal would often turn left rather than right if it happened not to be hungry. Others again would think that expectancy implies disappoint-

ment, with probable consequences in angry and aggressive behaviour, if the expected event does not happen. Yet other meanings might be attached to the word 'expectancy': perhaps it can
only be used in this example because food is something of which
the animal has need. It might be held that one does not 'expect'
something to which one is indifferent. And so on. Almost any
group of these interpretations may be the ones understood by some
particular person when he hears the word. One must therefore
specify precisely which meanings are intended to apply, which
involves saying what the animal's behaviour will be in certain
other circumstances. Whether we are asking people to report what
goes on in their minds, or whether we are using as explanations of
action words created in everyday life, we must define what is
meant in terms of observed events: that is, situations to which a
man must respond, and actions or words which he produces.
Without such definition there can be no agreement between different investigators.

This then is the attitude of the modern behaviourist: he does not
confine himself simply to studying non-verbal actions, but he does
insist on taking into account the operations by which any particular observation is made. This means rejecting concepts which
are not defined by any operation; rejecting a man's statements
about his experience unless his words have been given some un-
ambiguous meaning. So we reach the view of a science which
relates events at the bodily senses ('stimuli') to events at those
parts of the body which act on the outer world ('responses').
Amongst responses, it is perfectly legitimate to include the statements made by human beings, as long as the differences between
such responses correspond to differences between other stimuli or
other responses.

## Objections

Three objections may be made to this view. The first is 'But such
a science already exists and is called physiology'. The second is
'But such a science cannot be constructed because behaviour is too

variable'. The third is 'But such a science is not worth constructing because the important aspects of Man are precisely those which cannot be communicated'. Each of these objections is worth considering, so we had better take each in turn before concluding this chapter.

Physiology, the study of the functions of the body, is indeed closely connected with the study of behaviour. As we shall see, some behaviourists have gone too far in asserting their independence of the adjacent science: one cannot discuss stimuli and responses without any reference to the nervous system through which they are connected. It is equally true that studying the function of nerves is unreal without studying the chemical changes which take place as an impulse travels along a nerve. That is, physiology depends on biochemistry just as behaviour theory depends on physiology, no more and no less. In modern times a useful analogy to the distinction between behaviour and nervous function is to be found in the realm of engineering. The control system of a crane, a guided missile, or a ship may be arranged in different ways. The crane may respond directly to movements of the control handle, or respond only after a time-lag; there may be stabilizing 'feed-back' which detects any departure from the speed selected by the controller, and corrects it automatically; and so on. It is meaningful to discuss these general features of a control without considering whether the mechanism underlying it is mechanical, hydraulic, or electronic. Naturally this is not to say that the details of the mechanism are unimportant, but they are to some extent a separate matter. Very often electronic control systems can be substituted for mechanical ones, provided that their behaviour is the same. Still more, one kind of valve or circuit can be substituted for another if other details are altered to keep the behaviour of the whole system the same. The behaviour of one kind of system can be simulated by another – it is possible to arrange on the ground an electronic linkage between aircraft controls and instruments, which causes the latter to show precisely the same readings as would appear in flight when the same controls were moved. Many engineers are in fact occupied in studying these behavioural properties of complex engineering systems, as matters of importance by themselves and abstracted from the particular valves and levers which embody them. Equally psychology studies the general patterns of control in the nervous system, for example the presence or absence of time-lags between stimulus and response, or the evidence for self-correcting mechanisms which keep animal actions on a constant course despite the interference of the environment. As the analogy shows, the boundaries between psychology and physiology are apt to become blurred, and it is wise for people in each science to know what is happening in the other: but the distinction is still a real one. It is especially important to keep it alive in the case of biological systems as opposed to engineering ones, because the engineer is not usually faced with a completed system designed by somebody else. He knows what he wants his devices to do and so chooses appropriate hydraulic, electronic, or other details to bring about the right result. In the biological case we do not usually know what the nervous system does, and if we try to unravel the details of its working without knowing the general outline, we are likely to get lost. To study the physiology of the nervous system without first studying what it does is as hopeful as to try reconstructing the rules of a game such as chess by examining the board and the pieces; it might be done but it would require superhuman ability to guess correctly.

Psychology is thus distinct from physiology: but there is still the second objection 'Is it possible?' There is only one answer to this, and it is simply to try. One experience is universal, however, amongst those who are persuaded to try experiments on behaviour; and that is an access of confidence in the predictability of the results. In everyday life we rarely see several people or animals meeting exactly the same situations. Even so, we do rely on uniformity to some extent, and are surprised if we see a man wearing a tartan shirt with evening dress or learning a new language within a day. In deliberately contrived situations, the consistency

43

of behaviour becomes more marked, because chance changes in background circumstances are reduced. Of course, there remains a degree of variability in a biological system which is greater than that in, say, a Diesel engine: but as we shall see in the next chapter, this appears to be because the brain makes use of chance variations in behaviour just as the process of evolution makes use of chance variations in the combination of hereditary qualities. It has been possible to produce a science of genetics, although that science deals largely with chance processes: equally it is possible to state principles of learning. Whether we shall ultimately reach a limit beyond which the consistency of behaviour disappears, we cannot tell: but there is no way to find out without trying, and our experience so far is hopeful.

This leads on to the third objection, that any results obtained by this method are not worthwhile, since it is the quality of his experience which makes Man so valuable, and this cannot be communicated in the language of science. This objection is attractive since it seems to appeal to our sense of the worth and dignity of human beings: but unhappily it does not take sufficiently seriously the meaning of the word 'incommunicable'. It is not only scientific language which requires agreement between speaker and listener, but all language. Certainly that agreement need not always be established in the scientific way in which one specifies the exact types of light to which a given observer says 'I see blue'. It is also possible for a talented person to express novel experience by relating it to words whose meaning his audience knows from other situations. Nevertheless he transmits his private message only by translating it into public terms. It is only those messages, which cannot be translated in this way, that lie outside the possible boundaries of the behaviourist. If therefore we reject the scientific approach because it is not private, we are also rejecting all attempts to share in the experience of others, whether artistic, religious, or of some other kind. Is it not egocentric to have no curiosity concerning the richness and variety of other people, and are we not lacking in humility and sensitivity if we take no care to disentangle the mysteries of their nature? The scientific path is not the only one: but all ways, which do not assume that all men have the same experience, rely ultimately on the description of situations and actions. That is, upon the data which the behaviourist uses.

It might still be argued that, although all knowledge of other men must indeed use the same sources as the behaviourist does, that knowledge can never be certain except by destroying morality and responsibility. If we establish a perfect relation between stimulation and response, this argument would run, we leave no room for freedom: the search for such relations is self-contradictory, since the psychologists who pursue it must choose to do so. This argument also is fallacious. It assumes that the only type of cause which can influence behaviour is one which affects individual actions directly: as, for instance, when a particular gesture is ascribed to hereditary influences, and the person who makes it is unable to change its character. It is equally possible for heredity and environment to act in a different way, to produce a complex system which will control its own detailed actions. Human ingenuity can now produce control devices for chemical processes, and these devices will adapt themselves to circumstances by changing the method of control which they use, until they produce a more effective result. It is impossible for the designer to predict the behaviour of such a machine, since its actions are not laid down specifically in its construction. There is no contradiction in attaching words such as 'responsibility' to a self-regulating system, since once it is launched it is its own master: and yet we may well seek out the principles by which its regulation is achieved. In theological terms, to say that a creature has free will does not make it any the less a creature, deriving its being from sources outside itself. It would be idle to pretend that we now know the detailed way in which the machinery of moral choice revolves: but we do at least know that important animal or human actions do not follow single isolated outside causes as a billiard ball moves in response to a blow of a cue. No future discoveries will reverse that fact, or turn man from a complex system into a simple one.

Part of the difficulty felt by men of goodwill, in approving a scientific approach to human beings, may be due to a confusion of factual and procedural statements. That is, they may take the sentence 'I believe in the dignity and value of human beings' as a remark of the same type as 'I believe Edinburgh to be about three hundred miles from London'. If both sentences were indeed of the same kind, then the first belief, like the second, could be disproved by some contrary evidence. In fact this cannot be done, any more than one can disprove the belief expressed in the sentence 'I believe in using miles rather than kilometres to measure distance'. Procedural statements define the rules which are going to govern our speech or action: factual statements make assertions within the limits set by the procedural ones, and can be contradicted by showing that the procedure to which they appeal does not confirm them. Stating the mileage between Edinburgh and London is an appeal to an agreed procedure for measuring mileage and so can be true or false: preferring miles to kilometres is itself a procedure and can only be combated by such means as argument and the demonstration of practical consequences. In English both kinds of statement may start 'I believe' and so give rise to considerable confusion: nevertheless there is no doubt of their logical distinction, which is sometimes expressed in the case of language by referring to procedural statements as belonging to a 'metalanguage' and not to the original language at all. One is not therefore appealing to some mystical intuition when one says that moral and religious attitudes cannot be disproved by experimental results on behaviour. So there is no justification for rejecting the behaviourist approach to people because it might be inconsistent with these moral and religious attitudes which are felt as having an immediate and prior claim. It is indeed true that adequate understanding of behaviour will make any moral attitude more effective: if we wish to produce a society of saints, it would be useful to know whether the methods of Billy Graham are more likely to have this effect than the methods of St Thomas

Aquinas were. On a more concrete level, if we wish to reduce transport accidents we ought to know whether a given sum will produce the biggest reduction when spent on propaganda, on improved control systems, or on prosecuting individuals who are involved in accidents. But the same psychological knowledge could be used to spread Fascism or secure the greatest profit for some individual or clique. Knowledge about behaviour is as ethically neutral as knowledge about the atom, which can be used either for power stations or for bombs. As with nuclear power, however, to refuse knowledge about behaviour has ethical implications just as much as the use of that knowledge does. Men in ignorance of their nature are not therefore free: they are controlled by the unknown and inhuman forces of environment and heredity in ways which we do not fully understand and therefore cannot combat. In some parts of the world men resist the advance of drainage because they fear the harmful magic that may be done by enemies possessing the products of their bodies: in other places lovely and sensitive craftsmanship dies out when machine products become available. Mental illness acounts for a high proportion of our hospital beds; and we are all threatened by the dangers of a clash between one society and another. Under these circumstances it is surely urgent to acquire knowledge so that we can make our moral attitudes effective, whether those attitudes are humanist or Christian.

## The Topics to be Met

After calling up the image of the human suffering which is due to our ignorance of psychology, and after spending much time in arguing that there is no other way (besides the behaviourist one) of attaining certain knowledge of other men, it may seem strange to say that most of this book will deal with animal behaviour. There are several reasons for this. In the first place, many of our arguments have shown that our methods of approach to animals are not as different as might be thought from those of investigating men. Since animals can be brought up under controlled conditions they have a number of advantages as experimental subjects. Secondly, the essence of our attitude is that man should be seen in his biological setting. But thirdly and most important, there is one difference between modern behaviourism and Watson's, which has not yet been mentioned. Nowadays we are more modest, and do not make claims to understand all human behaviour in terms of such simple principles as the view of conditioning mentioned earlier. Great importance is attached now to the limiting conditions outside which a theory is not expected to hold. Theories for rats do not apply to species possessing, for example, language. Naturally, since men are more complicated than other species are, our knowledge about them is split up into a number of small areas without much inter-connection. We know a good deal about the learning of meaningless nonsense material, about the perception of colours and to some extent of shapes, about fatigue in prolonged work and so on: but to discuss each of these areas would give a very fragmented and unclear picture of the whole. Amongst the simpler animals it is easier to form a general view, even although much still remains to be learned. The lessons drawn from them apply to some extent to man, although other principles need to be added to deal with human behaviour. The knowledge we have so far, however, will serve merely as an example of the technique which is being applied, and which will lead to more adequate theories in the future; there is no substitute for prolonged study if we want to find answers to the practical problems mentioned at the end of the last section.

In the next chapter we will discuss animal learning and its relation to the evolution of species. There are two major difficulties in this field – the effects of punishment and the appearance of sudden correct responses with no previous errors – and these will be dealt with in the two following chapters. From this point we will turn to two contrasting views of scientific method: should psychologists produce specific theories and test them, or rather gather facts without theories? Each view has its supporters, and examples of profitable research to uphold its case.

Next we will look at experiments on the effect of brain injury on learning: and then at the motives which seem important in animal behaviour. By that time we should be able to form some opinion of the success of the behaviourist approach so far. But until we come to that final stage, we may abandon philosophical arguments and turn rather to experiment.

# 2

# The Evolutionary View

Most animals are well adapted to the circumstances in which they live. Creatures who live amid ice and snow, like Polar bears, are often white in colour, with the result that they are hard to see: animals from more temperate climates, such as the ordinary English rabbit, are more suitably coloured for the background against which they are likely to live. It is now almost universally held that this adjustment to the environment takes place by a process of evolution through natural selection. In any particular time and place the individual members of a species are not completely identical, but rather show a range of differences. The children of an individual are more likely to resemble him than to be like some other individual picked at random. If then the species lives in a place where a certain type of physique is an asset, the individuals possessing that type of body will be more likely to survive and to have children, and the next generation will contain a higher proportion of individuals with the useful characteristics. Eventually the species will consist very largely of animals who have the useful type of physique, and other kinds of individual will be the exception.

An example which is often quoted because of its neatness is the change in the predominant colour of moths in England since the Industrial Revolution. Certain species of moth can be found in both dark and light coloured forms. In the smokier parts of the country the dark form is the more common, while in the West the situation is reversed. Direct experiments have shown that when a sample of marked moths of both colours is released in an industrial area, more of the dark ones survive than of the light, largely because the latter are seen and eaten by birds. In a smoke-free area the dark moths are more conspicuous and so suffer more losses from the birds.

In this way, as we believe, the present bewildering array of animal forms has developed. But behaviour also can be inherited, presumably by the handing on of some structure in the nervous system, so that the individual will have an inborn tendency to behave in a certain way. If a particular kind of behaviour confers some advantage, there will continue to be individuals with that kind of behaviour, and it may become universal in a species. For example, baby herring gulls will open their mouths wide when shown a rough model of a bird's head with a red dot on the beak. The adult gull does have such a red dot: and therefore when the parent comes back to the nest with food for his little ones he finds open mouths awaiting him. It is easy to see that if an individual herring gull was born without this inherited behaviour he would breakfast rather poorly while in the nest with more normal birds: the response to the red dot gives an advantage and so the individuals who possessed it survived, had children, and passed the response on to them. Another example is the effect produced by a model of a Sea Eagle upon the geese which might normally be victims for such a bird of prey. As the model is moved overhead they take avoiding action: one can well see that individuals without this response have tended through the years to be noticed and eaten, and so have not produced offspring.

More complex still are such processes as mating and nest-building. As any observant person will know, different kinds of bird build different nests adapted to the type of surroundings which the particular species inhabits. Constructing such a nest is a lengthy operation involving a number of stages: but it is obvious that having a nest favours the survival of the young, and so birds with an inherited tendency to build nests have naturally become common. (There may be a learned element in nest-building, as well as an innate one, but for the moment we will include the capacity to learn the behaviour under the general label 'a tendency to build nests'.) Mating also is highly complex in many species, involving a long ritual of movements and postures before the act itself. Sometimes the process is so elaborate as to seem pointless: the peacock's display of his tail, or the bower bird's construction of an almost aesthetic pattern of leaves and flowers which the female inspects before mating, are obvious examples. But courtship rituals have several different kinds of advantage. They ensure that the partners mating are of the same species and so will stand a better chance of fertility. Even within the species they distinguish appropriate from inappropriate individuals: an immature bird will not court or respond to courtship as an adult would, and this will prevent a wasted mating. In some cases, furthermore, courtship may weed out defective individuals. Experiments on fruit-flies have shown that inbred males, who are less fertile, are often re- · jected by females during the courtship. In fruit-flies the courtship takes the form of a rapid side-to-side dance of both partners facing each other. It is likely that an inbred male does not keep up properly with the female, and so does not provide the stimulation she needs before accepting the male. From her point of view this is just as well, since she thus avoids an inferior mate.

We can see that natural selection would favour animals having these complex forms of behaviour, just as it would favour such reactions as gaping at the sight of a red dot. But the actual mechanism necessary to produce the more complex behaviour cannot be as simple as the minimum required to explain gaping. When the image of a red dot falls on the eye, messages travel along the nerves into the brain: and if we want to explain gaping we need only imagine that the incoming messages are there switched to travel out again to particular muscles. The particular connections between nerves which produce the switching might be established by heredity. But in the case of many species, mating (or for that matter nest-building, killing prey for food, and a large number of other activities) is not simply an action in response to a stimulus. If a mate, a prey, or material for a nest are not available when the need for them arises, the animal will move about the available territory until they are found: showing 'appetitive' behaviour, as it is called. Even when the desired object is found, several different approaches may need to be tried before it is attained. The first attack on the quarry may not kill it, or the possible mate may fail to respond to the first attempt at courtship. Such difficulties are met by repeated trials by the animal until the final and fairly stereotyped stage of the behaviour is reached, the actual mating or the eating of food. Following this 'consummatory act', as it is called, it is likely that some quite different form of behaviour will appear.

How can such a series of actions be inherited? It is not a mechanical push-button affair as gaping to a red dot might be. And it certainly does not depend on the kind of processes which go on inside human beings when they are scheming to attain some end. A long-standing example of the difference between intelligent and instinctive behaviour is that of a kind of solitary wasp which drags its prey to the entrance of its nest, then leaves it there while it enters and makes sure all is well inside, and finally emerges to drag in its supply of food. If an experimenter moves the prey away from the nest while the wasp is inside, the wasp will bring it back as soon as its absence is noticed. But the wasp will not then drag the body inside; it will leave it at the door again and have another look inside the nest before taking it in. If the prey is again removed during this absence, the whole cycle is repeated. A patient experimenter can keep this routine going for a long time. Similar absurdities can be produced in a number of these inborn types of behaviour, and they show quite clearly that the mechanism underlying the action is not that we normally call intelligence, and it does not profit from experience.

We must think rather of some bodily state inside the animal which causes its behaviour to change and vary until the consummatory act can be performed. Thus after being deprived of food the animal will be impelled to variable activity until it eats. It will move about, look in various places, and be generally restless: and only food will quieten it. The process does not require conscious foresight in the animal, any more than the white colour of the Polar bear requires a deliberate attempt on the part of the bear to make itself invisible. Just as bears with dark coats die out through being too conspicuous, actions which do not lead to food are abandoned and others attempted.

It should of course be noted that no animal behaves in a fashion which is completely random during the period of unsatisfied appetitive behaviour. Different species have different repertoires of actions, and an animal will only try those actions which happen to be in his repertoire when he is under the influence of a 'drive' such as hunger. A hawk may try various movements in attacking his prey: but he is not likely to try the actions which a hunting wasp would use. He is not even very likely to try the same movements that he would use in a courting situation. Nevertheless within a range of actions the hawk will use first one and then another until the end is achieved.

There are therefore two kinds of behaviour which may be inherited; prescribed reactions which appear to certain stimuli, and a more flexible type of performance in which different alternatives are tried in turn until the animal reaches a particular state or goal. (The two kinds may not be divided by a sharp line, but rather merge into one another: however, it is useful to distinguish them to get our ideas clear when talking about instinctive behaviour.) Either kind may help the survival of animals which possess it, and so become common through evolution. The more flexible type has the advantage that animals possessing it are adjusted to a wider range of situations in the outer world. If a bird's nest-building was completely dependent on the stimulus of seeing a certain kind of hole, the absence of that kind of hole in a district would mean the end of nest-building. This does not happen because birds will vary their behaviour, and use different kinds of location for their nest if they cannot achieve a nest in the preferred way. A change of vegetation in a district need not mean that a species of birds is reduced to a few who happen to have the correct reflexes: many individuals will produce adequate behaviour to meet the new conditions.

The flexible kind of mechanism therefore has some advantage over a fixed stimulus-response linkage, and this makes it reasonable that it should be widespread. But we must remember that even this kind of mechanism has its limits. As we have described it so far, it would respond with no greater efficiency on the thousandth appearance of some problem situation than it would on the first. In either first or thousandth case, various alternatives would be tried and eventual success achieved, but the speed of that success would remain the same. Remember the wasp and its repetition of the same sequence over and over again. Everyday observation of animals, let alone formal experiment, tells us that their behaviour contains more than this. They can profit from experience, so that they approach a familiar situation differently from a novel one. In the last chapter, we described Watson's attempt to explain this effect of learning, by supposing that a response made when a certain stimulus is present will in future be more likely to appear when that stimulus occurs. Experiment showed that this was not an adequate theory, because the response which is ultimately learned may not have been the one which happened most often when the particular stimulus was present. In the early Thirties therefore another theory of learning was put forward, and this we shall now consider.

## The Law of Effect

As we have said, there are certain states in which an animal will vary its behaviour in a restless and changeable fashion; and for each of these states there is an appropriate consummatory act which puts an end to the varied appetitive behaviour. Taking food, mating, nest-building, are consummatory in this sense. So also is escape from an unpleasant situation: a cat shut in a cage with a simple latch on the door will often become agitated and make various movements until it happens to knock the latch open and get out. Once outside, the agitation naturally dies away. Now just before the turn of the century it was noticed by an experimenter named Thorndike that cats who had been put in such a cage again and again did not take as long to get out as they did on their first experience of the problem. Thorndike argued that the action just before escaping from the cage was somehow boosted in priority by the escape: so that particular action became more likely to be tried next time the animal found itself in the cage. Since each escape would produce another rise in the probability of the 'correct' action, that act would happen sooner and sooner until the cat was able to escape from the cage immediately on being put in it.

This 'Law of Effect' was thought of as completely mechanical. A potter can mould a piece of clay into various shapes one after another but the last shape before the clay is fired in a kiln becomes the permanent shape of that piece of clay. The firing fixes the shape, and in a rather similar way the reward of escaping from the cage was supposed to fix a connection between the stimulus of being in the box and the response of undoing the latch. The Law of Effect is indeed very similar, in the field of learning, to the principle of natural selection in the evolution of species. Since individual animals differ, and those with useful characteristics survive and pass them on to their children, we can explain the delicate adjustment of each animal's shape to its surroundings without requiring a conscious purpose on the part of the Polar bear to grow a white coat. Equally each individual animal, on the theory we are considering, tries various actions and those become more common which are followed by consummatory acts. The attraction both of natural selection and of the Law of Effect, to certain types of mind, is that they do not call on explanatory principles of a quite separate order from those used in the physical sciences. It is not surprising therefore that the Law of Effect had been seized on, not merely as a generalization which is true of animals under certain conditions, but also as a fundamental principle which would explain all adaptive behaviour. This did not happen at once: when Thorndike first reported his experiments the Law of Effect was merely one principle amongst others. Indeed at that time Watson had not raised his battle-standard, and the problems of cats in cages were secondary to those of conscious experience. But once behaviour rather than experience had become the centre of attention: once learning had become a central problem, and the original theory of learning advanced by Watson had been shown inadequate: then the Law of Effect began to be put forward as the keystone of theory. This step is associated above all with the name of Clark Hull, who in the Thirties erected a very detailed and specific theory of behaviour in which the Law of Effect was the central point. By doing so he took into account the various difficulties met by Watson's theory. On a Hullian view, one could regard the original theory of conditioning held by Watson as due merely to the historical accident that salivation rather than some other action was the behaviour being observed. Salivation being a response to food, it was likely to occur just before the dog ate, and therefore by the Law of Effect would in future be likely to appear again whenever the bell (signal of food) rang. Salivation was not attached to the bell simply because it happened when the bell was ringing, but rather because its appearance was followed by a consummatory act. In everyday language, the dog was rewarded for salivating.

Looked at in this way, Watson's difficulties are greatly reduced. Naturally the dog must be hungry, so that the food shall act as a reward. Naturally the response most often made in a situation need not be the one which is learned, since only rewarded responses are learned and the frequency of an unrewarded response does not help it to persist. A rat will therefore break even a persistent tendency to turn left in a maze, if one feeds it only after it turns right. As was said in the last chapter, the difficulty of Watson's theory was that animals are not easily taught foolish actions. The theory put forward by Hull explains why this should be so.

At the same time Hull's approach gave due weight to the peculiarities of appetitive behaviour, already mentioned in this chapter. Such workers as Tolman and Holt had established in the Twenties that animals deprived of some essential goal would engage, as we have seen, in continually changing behaviour until it was achieved. This purposive behaviour is objective, and can be seen in animals by anybody who cares to perform the experiment. Watson's neglect of motives and rewards had therefore gone too far, since behaviour as well as experience revealed their importance. Hull's theory included this new emphasis on needs and rewards: the deprived animal was said to be under the influence of a 'drive', and the reduction of a drive was the reward or 'reinforcement' which would make the immediately previous actions more likely to appear in future.

So at this stage we see a theory analogous to natural selection being put forward as a complete explanation of learning: when a response occurs during the action of a stimulus, and the combination is closely followed by reduction of a drive, that response will in future be more likely to occur to that stimulus. Thus randomly varying responses will be selected by reward, and only those most likely to secure satisfaction will survive. As we have seen, there is no doubt that this mechanism does work on occasion, and an animal (or a man for that matter) will learn by trial and error. We cannot account for all behaviour either by simple innate responses, or by the more complex combination of appetitive and consummatory behaviour. But is the Law of Effect sufficient for all forms of learning? Are there other laws for problems more subtle than the cat in the cage? In the rest of this chapter we shall be considering difficulties which have been raised for the Law of Effect: and there are some difficulties which are so complicated as to require chapters to themselves. Certain very general difficulties may be considered immediately, because they are so similar to arguments urged against the theory of natural selection in the evolution of species.

In the first place, there is the fact that an animal in a problem situation does not show a continuous range of behaviour covering all the possible actions in a completely chance fashion. It is likely to try one group of actions and then shift sharply to another group without ever trying anything in between. For instance, a cat in a cage may explore one side of the cage, and then turn systematically to the other, rather than bouncing about all over the available space. The same type of observation holds in the case of evolution: moths do not come in all possible shades between white and black, but rather in sharply distinct light and dark varieties. Darwin did not take account of this, and based his theory on the idea that all degrees of some quality would be present in the population. We now know that heredity normally works in distinct units – the children of a given moth have a certain probability of being light or dark, but none of being a mixture. It is only with qualities determined by very many 'genes' (units of heredity) that one finds these sharp distinctions disappearing. People come in all kinds of body size, because many genes affect that quality: but they either suffer from sickle-cell anaemia or they do not, because only one gene decides that. There is no halfway house in such cases.* It can be shown mathematically that this handing-on of hereditary qualities in separate chunks, which a given individual either has or lacks, is essential for natural selection to work properly: a completely even distribution of all qualities, which most people would call random, would not result in species adapting to changes in the environment. So we do not nowadays regard the fact that fruit-flies have either normal or tiny wings, without all possible sizes in between, as evidence against natural selection. Rather it is evidence for it.

In the same way one should not think of the cat in the cage as putting itself into positions chosen at random from all those which its limbs would physically be able to take up. Rather there are certain distinct possibilities, co-ordinated and sensible-looking movements, amongst which the cat will choose: and when one of

---

* Save that of being free from the disease oneself, but carrying the tendency to pass it on to one's children. Strictly speaking you need two genes to have the disease: if you only have one, you will not get the disease, but if your wife also has one gene your child may have two and get the disease.

these is successful it is the whole movement which becomes more probable, rather than simply the particular twitches of muscle which preceded the escape. Curiously enough, nobody seems to have applied to animal behaviour the mathematical arguments used in the evolution of species: but on a less rigorous level one can see that complete actions such as pressing or lifting bars are more likely to be successful in almost any situation than unco-ordinated thrashing about would be.

So it is reasonable that the trial part of the trial-and-error process should consist of sharply distinguished alternative actions.

A second very general difficulty in using the Law of Effect as a universal explanation is the speed with which learning sometimes takes place. There hardly seems time for the chance process of trial and error. The same snag has appeared in the evolution of species: the speed with which moths have become black in industrial Britain seems remarkable at first sight when one thinks that dark moths must first appear by chance, establish their advantage, and only then begin to displace the lighter ones. Bees navigate making use of the direction of the sun, an incredibly complex inborn performance which can be disrupted by taking the insects to the Southern Hemisphere where the sun follows a different path. Yet strains of bees which have lived South of the Equator for a fairly small number of generations can navigate adequately. Penicillin is a new drug: but already germs resistant to it are a problem.

When a population of animals is exposed to new conditions, it does not usually consist only of one variety of animal. Rather it contains traces of other varieties which possess some advantages in the old environment, but insufficient to cause these varieties to equal the frequency of the dominant one. For instance, even in non-industrial Britain there are some dark moths: they have their own merits which allow a steady small proportion of the dark individuals to survive even though they do not equal the lighter ones in numbers. As a result, as soon as conditions change, there are qualities present in the population ready to increase in number if they happen to be useful in the new circumstances. As soon as industries arise, dark moths are there to increase in frequency. The speed with which a population of animals will adapt to change is not therefore so surprising: there need be no wait until new varieties happen to arise, because they are already present in small numbers. A particular illustration of this can be produced by maintaining two populations of fruit-flies at the same temperature: one population being inbred and the other outbred. The inbred strain will be as well adjusted to the prevailing temperature as the other strain will. But the outbred strain contains traces of qualities which have been lost in the inbred population, so that if the temperature is changed the two strains will not suffer equally. The inbred strain will drop severely in numbers, while the other will readjust rapidly to the new conditions.

In the same way the rapid learning of animals is often clearly due to the presence of a variety of already learned responses which are immediately available for the selective influence of the Law of Effect. An animal which has never previously been used for a learning experiment makes a very poor showing: and even when it has solved one problem it takes a long time to solve another. But in a long series of experiments by Harlow it has been shown that animals which have solved a number of problems become very quick at solving new ones. They may even learn a new problem after only one reward for the correct response. The need to train the animal, by building up a set of alternative responses, before it will adapt rapidly to a change in the problem is an amusing parallel to the effects of outbreeding. In both cases a foundation of variety is necessary before rapid adjustment can be made.

These rather general difficulties, then, need not rule out the Law of Effect, although they make us remember that the behaviour of an animal faced with a problem (such as escaping from a cage) is not a completely unorganized confusion. More serious objections come from three main fields of experiment, each of which we shall now examine. These experiments, intended to find the weak points in the Law of Effect, study firstly failures to learn even when a reward is given. Secondly there are investigations of learning when no reward is given. Thirdly, there are experiments in which reward is given for one action and another action seems to be learned. So each of these groups of experiments claims to produce facts which are not consistent with the general idea that learning is based on reward.

## The Attempts to Show Absence of Learning after Reward

At first sight it may seem that everyday experience makes it absurd to look for cases in which reward produces no effect. Surely we all do what brings us reward? But a little more thought will reveal a few cases in which this is not so: we do not always repeat successful acts when we do not know quite what it was we did that was right. If we are given a reward without being told why, it might not influence our behaviour. Of course, this may be a peculiar feature of human beings, and merely part of the complex superstructure erected in our own species over the simple principles of behaviour present in lower animals. But if, say, rats could be shown to be uninfluenced by rewards given under conditions which make the connection of reward and action unclear, then we would have reason to be rather doubtful of the Law of Effect as a basic principle.

Now at about the same time that the importance of reward was being driven home to animal experimenters, an investigator named Krech showed that rats learning mazes do not explore them in an unpredictable way. They act in a way which we would describe in humans as showing that they set up theories or hypotheses of the way the maze is set out. For instance, if some alleys in a maze are lit up and some are dark, one can often observe the rat turning systematically into every lighted alley; even though the light bears no real relation to the correct path through the maze. After trying the lighted alleys for a while, the animal will give up this system and take up another. For instance, it may take the right-hand path at every turning, although this too is not the true solution to the problem of getting through the maze. This behaviour looks like that which an intelligent man might adopt as a way of tackling the maze methodically, without the random trial and error supposed by the Law of Effect. None the less, the finding that rats make systematic series of responses of one type, act on 'hypotheses' to use Krech's term, is not in itself an argument against the Law. One could easily argue that the approach response had at some past time happened to be rewarded when it occurred to a lighted alley, and so was temporarily more likely to appear than any other. After appearing for a time, it would die away in strength through absence of reward, and the next strongest tendency would take its place. So the animal would not simply try any action at random, but behave systematically in one way and another until the correct responses became the strongest. That action would be the most regularly rewarded and so would not die away as others had done. Hypothesis behaviour by itself is not evidence against the Law of Effect.

But Krech claimed a further analogy between the animal's behaviour and that of a man acting on a hypothesis. A human being who wanders about in the Hampton Court maze trying the right-hand turn at every junction will eventually decide that his hypothesis does not lead to success. But he is not likely to know the correct path through the maze: he probably stands little better chance of success, on his next entry into it, than a man would who had never been to Hampton Court before. When you and I are trying favourite hypotheses, we do not notice evidence inconsistent with our theories to anything like the same extent that we do when in an open frame of mind. If this were true of the rat also then if, acting on the hypothesis that lighted alleys are correct, he turns right into a lighted alley and is rewarded, that reward will not strengthen his tendency to turn right but only his hypothesis that lighted alleys are correct.

How can one test this analogy and so show that a reward given after an action does not always make that action more probable?

The way which has most often been used is to put the rat over and over again into a simple maze shaped like a T, and to reward it with, say, food for turning right at the junction. Before the animal shows any sign of having learned this response, one changes the treatment by rewarding only left turns instead. Then one compares the rate of learning of the rat with that of others who have been rewarded for turning left all through the experiment, from their first meeting with the maze. If the Law of Effect is strictly true, the rats who were originally rewarded for turning right will find it hard to learn to turn left. If the other view is correct, the early rewards for turning right will have had no effect since the rat was then acting on some quite different hypothesis and would not have noticed that right turns were rewarded. So on this other view the rat should learn just as fast whichever kind of treatment it had received.

Some early experiments claimed to find no difference between groups trained in these two ways, which would, as we have said, show that learning is discontinuous, changing abruptly as hypotheses are taken up and discarded. Unfortunately there is a clash of evidence here: for later experimenters did establish that animals who were first rewarded for doing one thing and then for doing the opposite learned more slowly than did those who were always rewarded for the same action. These later experimenters made various technical criticisms of the earlier work, and in general used simple and rigorous methods which have probably caused most people to accept their findings rather than the earlier ones. For instance, they took great care to balance out all initial preferences of the animals for one arm or other of the T maze. So the general feeling has been that the Law of Effect has had the best of this 'continuity controversy', as it is called.

Very recently, however, some doubt has been expressed about this feeling. The later experiments might support continuity of learning not because they were better experiments but because they put the animal in rather a different situation. As one simplifies the maze, and trains the animal out of any habits it may bring to the problem, one leaves the rat with few alternatives to consider: whereas a more complex maze leaves a number of possibilities open. It is not too surprising that in simple situations a rat might act on one hypothesis and yet be able to take note of a few facts relevant to some other hypothesis. In more complex cases perhaps there would be too much for the animal to take in, and so it would confine its attention to the hypothesis on which it happened to be acting.

Let us take an analogy from human behaviour. If you put a glove on your right hand, hold a penny in it, and then hold out both fists to a friend and ask him to choose, he can have no rational basis for choice and must pick a hand at random. Suppose he chooses the right hand: in that case he will win. Next time you may put the glove on the left hand, but hold the penny still in the right. If he goes on the hypothesis that the gloved hand is correct, he will lose. But it is very likely that even while acting on that incorrect hypothesis, and so losing, he will notice that the right hand is always rewarded—because there are very few alternatives to take into account. If on the other hand you face your friend with a choice between two hands, one gloved and one not, one right and one left, one palm downwards and one not, one with the little finger extended and one not, one held above waist height and one below, and if you change these features about on successive trials so that no two are consistently associated: he is not likely to notice which feature goes regularly with the penny until he guesses the correct one and tries responding to it. In the language of telephone engineers, the situation presents more information than a man's limited capacity can handle. He therefore selects some of the information and discards the rest.

One experimenter has tried making the turnings of a maze look different in several different ways, so that there are several possible alternatives for the rat to consider. Learning is slower in this case than it is when the maze alleys are the same in all but one or two features. The rat is also more likely to show hypothesis behaviour rather than trying the alleys unsystematically. So far as these results go, it looks as though learning may be continuous only in very simple situations and become discontinuous if the problem is a complex one. But the evidence is not very firm: there need to be more studies of the effect of making a maze complex, and as yet the Law of Effect is not seriously shaken by this group of experiments.

There is another rather different line of attack which has definitely shown failure to learn even after reward. This is the method of teaching an animal to react to a complex pattern of stimuli and then presenting part of the pattern by itself. For instance, one might condition some response to the sound of a musical note, and then play a tune which incidentally contained that note. The response would not appear, just as the reader probably did not notice the word 'dent' embedded in a word of the last sentence. A number of experiments of this type have been performed, particularly using visual patterns and testing for response to elements of the pattern in isolation. It is very often found that part of the pattern by itself will not produce the response, although that response was rewarded previously in the presence of those stimuli. This fact is generally admitted, and those who believe in the Law of Effect therefore add some gloss to their phrasing of it, to the effect that the rewarded response is only learned to the complete pattern of stimuli which were present during learning – or at least to a very considerable part of the pattern. It is probably fair to say that this modification of the Law of Effect is not a serious one.

## The Attempts to Show Learning Without Reward

If our everyday experience needs rather careful examination for cases in which we fail to learn even though rewarded, the same is not true for the opposite kind of case. There are many occasions when we learn without any immediate and obvious reward. Casually looking from the window of a bus, we may notice a restaurant and learn its position without ever going in and being fed: glancing through a dictionary we may learn the meaning of some unusual word which catches our eye, without having any immediate use for it. Experiments on similar situations with animals have correspondingly been more numerous than those on the continuity controversy.

A very simple type of experiment is worth considering first, because it shows both the line of attack on the Law of Effect, and also the kind of answer which the supporters of the Law make to these attacks. The experiment is that known as 'sensory preconditioning'. In this we ring a bell and flash a light, both together, in the presence of a dog. The combination is repeated over and over again. Then we condition a response to one of the signals, say to the light. After the conditioning we ring the bell, and look to see if the conditioned response occurs. The result usually reported is that it does, but not very strongly, and it seems that this is not a very good way of teaching the animal to respond to the bell. All the same if there is any learning at all, there seems to be a breach of the Law of Effect: for the bell has never occurred just before a rewarded response. In everyday language, the dog remembers that the bell goes with the light, and has been rewarded for responding to the light, so when it hears the bell it reacts. But words such as 'remember' or 'memory' cannot fairly be used about animals, because they are rough descriptions of processes in human beings and whatever the corresponding events may be in the rat, they will certainly be much simpler. From one point of view, the whole problem discussed in this chapter concerns the nature of the fundamental mechanism on which 'memory' is based. The Law of Effect suggests that reward is essential for the counterpart of memory in animals: other theories deny this, and suggest that events are somehow stored in the animal's head regardless of the presence or absence of reward. Sensory preconditioning is thus evidence against the Law of Effect because the vital connection between bell and light has never been rewarded.

To this, supporters of the Law of Effect can reply that some reward might be present which the experimenter cannot detect. A reward need not be only food, water, a mate, or a similar direct primary goal: but also can be any stimulus associated with such a goal. If a rat is used to finding food in a particular kind of box, it will learn problems merely in order to be allowed to get at that kind of box. This kind of 'secondary reinforcement' might be present in experiments claiming to be on learning without reward. The dog may have learned some tenuous connection between light and food in his everyday life, so that when bell and light occur together the connection between them can be built up through the secondarily rewarding properties of the light, without any infringement of the Law of Effect. So long as sensory preconditioning produces only scanty learning and is hard to demonstrate, which it admittedly is, the necessity of reward for learning can still be held as a general doctrine.

There is another kind of experiment on learning without reward which is much less easy to counter. This is the 'latent learning' experiment, in which an animal is repeatedly allowed to explore a maze containing food when he is not hungry: and then made hungry and put into the maze. Under these circumstances the rat behaves as we ourselves do with the restaurant seen from the window of a bus: as long as we have no need of a restaurant our behaviour shows no sign that we know where it is, but if we become hungry when in the neighbourhood we will seek out the restaurant. In similar style the rat wanders through the maze with little sign of learning until he is made hungry; and then he runs to the food. Within a few trials he is getting through the maze as fast as a rat who has been hungry throughout his experience of the maze. In other words, our experimental rat has learned a good deal about the maze when he was not hungry and was therefore presumably getting no reward from finding his way through it.

It is important to be clear that this experiment cannot be explained as easily as sensory preconditioning can. Secondary rewards could indeed be present: in fact, as we have just described the experiment, they must be quite definitely so, since there will be the sight and smell of food and the animal can probably never be completely satiated to the point where no reward value at all attaches to the food. But the whole point of the experiment is the sharp change in behaviour when the animal is made hungry. The previous learning cannot have been a weak and inferior process, because of the high level of performance of the hungry rat: and yet this learning did not affect performance until the animal was hungry. The learning and the performance are separate, and so far everything we have said about the Law of Effect supposed them to be identical.

The separation fits nicely into the views of E. C. Tolman, who, like Hull and Lashley, is one of the great names of the period. He regarded learning a maze as the formation of a kind of map inside the rat, requiring no reward to be successfully accomplished. Even an animal which had a perfect map, however, need show no sign of its knowledge in behaviour until some purpose caused a point on the map to become a goal, whereupon the animal would proceed to that point. This kind of approach has been throughout the Thirties and Forties the main alternative to the Law of Effect doctrine with which Hull's name is associated. As we shall see neither side can be said to have won the contest, but each has had its local victories. The field of latent learning is one of Tolman's victories; in the later theories of Hull and of his supporter and successor Spence a distinction is made between learning and performance. This is done by saying that the probability of a response is related to the number one gets by multiplying together the strength of drive (hunger, thirst, etc.) and the strength of the habit (the amount which has been learned). As the result of multiplying anything by 0 is equal to 0, this means that in the absence of drive there will be no response even though the habit is strongly established. Conversely, of course, even a strongly motivated animal is not likely to make the right response until it has learned it. In order to calculate the strength of the habit, one merely looks at the number of times that particular response has been rewarded. One does not take into account the strength of the reward. So there can be complete learning where there is only a tenuous reward, but the act learned will only appear when it is needed.

This revised Hull-Spence approach can perhaps be illustrated by an analogy. The lighting of an electric light requires both the placing of a bulb in the socket and also a supply of current to the switch which controls the socket. Let us compare the turning of the switch to the presentation of a stimulus to an animal, and the lighting of the lamp to the appearance of a response. Then learning, the placing of the bulb in the socket, does not need much of a reward and will take place even when no drive is present – one can put a bulb in even if the electricity is turned off at the main. But turning on the mains supply is necessary if one wants the lamp to light: drive is necessary for response to appear even though the connection of stimulus and response has been established.

To summarize the conclusions of these experiments on learning without reward, it is now generally admitted that learning may occur with a very small amount of reward, as for example when the animal sees food when thoroughly fed. Such learning can be just as effective as learning with a normal reward, but it need not affect action until a drive is in operation. It is therefore primarily action rather than learning which depends on reward. The simple principles of the Law of Effect must be modified to take these results into account.

## Learning That as opposed to Learning How

If I am learning to ride a bicycle, it is reasonable to put forward the doctrine that certain of my actions are reinforced by success and become more probable. Gradually I acquire a tendency to turn the handlebars and lean appropriately when I feel the machine beginning to fall: and ultimately I know how to perform the skill. But much learning is of a different kind in which instead of learning how to do something I learn that something is the case. This latter type of learning may not cause me to repeat successful actions at all. For example, suppose I find an attractive restaurant by turning right out of Piccadilly when walking West. Next time I am hungry I may be walking East along the same street, and if so I shall certainly not turn right again since I know that the restaurant is now on my left. I will go to the same place in which I found the restaurant previously, even though this means producing some action that I have never used at all before, let alone had rewarded.

The same ability to find a place rather than repeat an action appears in rats. It has long been known that if they are taught a maze in the ordinary way, and if the maze is then filled with water, the rats will swim through it correctly. Yet this means that they are making responses which have never been directly rewarded in the past. An even more dramatic effect has been shown recently: rats can be pulled through a maze passively on a little trolley, and they will learn from this experience to run through the maze to food. In this case no action at all has taken place to be rewarded, and yet a successful response appears when the animal is put to the test.

This again is a result which does not fit the simple Law of Effect. It does of course, agree with Tolman's view mentioned a little earlier, that the animal forms a model or map inside its head and then acts on the information contained in this map. Tolman and his colleagues have in fact carried out on rats an experiment analogous to the situation of a man walking down Piccadilly in two different directions. They used a maze shaped like a cross, and taught the animal that if it started from, say, the South arm of the cross it should turn left to get food. If a trained rat was then started from the North arm of the cross it would turn right, as it should do to get to the same place: but turning right has never been rewarded. Naturally this experiment depends upon the maze being one in which the animal can see the outside world sufficiently to know that it is being started from the North rather than the South.

There are various modifications of the Law of Effect which will take these facts into account. For example, one could suggest that past experience has linked together some of the animal's actions before it ever entered this particular experiment. It will often have happened that the animal has seen something a long way off, walked, and found itself nearer the original stimulus. On other occasions it will have seen something, swum, and found itself nearer: or seen something, crawled, and found itself nearer. These various possible actions may have been linked by the similarity of these experiences, so that rewarding one of them tends to strengthen the others as well. If the circumstances are inappropriate for the action which was rewarded, the animal will perform one of the others. Thus it will swim if the maze is full of water, walk if it is not, turn in either direction according to the starting point, and so on. Another similar but slightly different modification of the Law of Effect would be to argue that the response most affected by reward is the internal response of 'seeing a particular place in the maze'. The animal then carries out whatever movements or actions will lead to this internal response. Saying this is very much the same as upholding Tolman's idea, that the rat has a map inside its head. But talking about the map as an internal response allows some people to feel that the general principles of the Law of Effect still apply. How far this is a real explanation of the learning of places rather than actions is rather debatable: we will come back to the problem in Chapter IV. For the moment it is enough to say that the fact, that place learning does occur, cannot be fitted into the simple Law of Effect we originally stated, but can possibly be taken into account by a complication of the Law.

Indeed, the conclusion from the three groups of experiments we have considered is that the Law is roughly true but requires a good deal of detailed qualification. To summarize what we have said, animals do seem to act systematically rather than behaving at random while they are still solving a problem. But the weight of the experimental evidence is that this does not prevent each reward for a correct action from having its effect. It is hard to find cases where learning fails to appear even when an action is rewarded. On the other hand, it is fairly easy to prove learning where the amount of reward must be very slight; and this means that we have to distinguish between the amount which has been learned and the actual tendency to act at any time. The amount learned seems to be just as great with only slight reward: but action does not take place unless it is worthwhile, that is, unless the reward is big enough. Finally, it has to be admitted that rewarding an animal for doing one thing in one set of circumstances may automatically teach him to do a quite different thing in other circumstances: he learns places and situations as well as actions, and although we can call this learning a rather special kind of action, it clearly is not the ordinary kind.

## Other Kinds of Reward Theory

The Law of Effect as advanced by Thorndike and later by Hull is only one of the possible hypotheses which could be put together using the general mechanism of evolutionary theory: random variation together with a selective agency. There are in fact a number of other variations on the same theme. It is worth mentioning some of them because no experiments have firmly ruled them out, and by their number they therefore show how many details remain to be settled when one makes the simple statement 'reward helps learning'.

One variation on the general principle is to argue that reward does not possess some special property of its own, but rather produces its undoubted effects by virtue of other and more fundamental laws. This is a view advanced by E. B. Guthrie, whose name was mentioned in the last chapter as an upholder of a sophisticated version of Watson's theory of learning. Watson believed that stimuli and responses became linked simply through happening at the same time. On Guthrie's view, learning does indeed take place whenever some action takes place in a given situation: but equally if a similar situation occurs again and the action is not repeated (perhaps because learning is not yet sufficiently advanced), the learning is reversed. The importance of reward is then that it changes the situation fundamentally so that unlearning cannot take place. Hearing a bell when you are hungry is not the same as hearing it when you have had food: if you tend to learn the last thing you did in a given situation, you will therefore

73

learn the last thing you did when you were hungry. Making some other marked change in the situation would do just as well, on this theory.

The usual verdict on Guthrie's view has been that it is too far detached from our present experimental knowledge to be proved or disproved. We are still asking whether reward has a general effect, and analysing that effect still further must wait until we are sure of its existence and limits. But there is a steady minority current of thought which holds that the theory has advantages even in our present state of knowledge.

Another variation on the Law of Effect is to deny that reward produces a gradual increase in the probability of an action. Rather one could say that sharp changes in probability occur either upwards or downwards if the state of the animal is outside prescribed limits; if, for example, it continues to be hungry. An animal might be dividing its time in certain proportions, between a number of activities, and one of these activities could be one which secures food. If that action is an infrequent one, the continued hunger would, on this theory, produce a sharp change in the way the animal spends its time: the first such sharp change might lead to a condition in which the right action was even less probable, and if so there would be another change, and another, and another until the right act happened and the changes ceased. On the average the animal would, if it operated in this way, end up spending more time in the correct activity. The result is much the same as on the original Law of Effect but the mechanism is different and if we plot rate of learning on a graph the type of curve would be different. This kind of theory has been put forward by Ross Ashby who has constructed a machine that adjusts itself in this way: but no experiments seem to have been done to test whether reward produces gradual systemative changes in probability or on the other hand puts a stop to series of sudden random changes.

Other theorists have worked out ways in which known physical or physiological systems could give rise to the Law of Effect. For instance, if one supposes a large number of nerve cells connected together, one can on various assumptions work out that successful outputs of the system of nerves will tend to be repeated. This kind of argument helps to reinforce the point that reward need not act in any mystical or super-physical way: but the value of theories of the physiology of the Law of Effect is strictly limited until we are sure that the Law really does hold.

## General Conclusion

The rough idea, that actions followed by reward are repeated, is one which is likely to occur to most intelligent people who think about possible explanations of behaviour. As we have seen, it is approximately true but must be stated very carefully. Some of the obvious possible theories, such as the idea that large and obvious rewards will be better than very indirect and concealed ones, have already been disproved by experiment. There remain a number of others which have not, and there are no good grounds for supporting one of them rather than another. Yet with these cautions it is still possible to think of behaviour as being adapted to the environment in the same way as anatomy is: it varies, and the successful variations are selected. This simple mechanism alone is obviously in need of help when it comes to explaining conflicts of motives, or anticipatory and insightful behaviour, and we can therefore turn now to examining some of the later bricks which have been laid on the foundation of the Law of Effect.

# 3

# Anxiety and Conflict

In the late Thirties the rapid success of the Law of Effect became overshadowed by an irritating but persistent difficulty. Besides rewards there are also punishments: things which an animal or a man will positively avoid rather than seek. Now at first sight the difference between reward and punishment is trivial. In both cases there is an unpleasant state originally (hunger, thirst, or some other drive in the one case, pain in the other) and the ending of this unpleasantness is the circumstance which produces learning. In the last chapter we actually used learning to escape from a puzzle-box as our introduction to the Law of Effect, and that example is one of relief from discomfort. Surely the ending of any unpleasant situation is in some sense a reward, whether we call the situation itself a drive or a punishment?

This argument is plausible so far as it goes, and it allows us to explain why an animal will learn to raise its paw to a signal whether we reward it by feeding it or by turning off an electric shock. But there is another possible way of arranging the experiment: we can 'reward' the animal by never giving the shock at all so long as it responds correctly. One can in fact make a direct comparison between two ways of teaching a response, both using shock. On the one hand the animal can be shocked every time, and be freed from this unpleasant experience each time it does the right thing. Or on the other hand, the shock could be delayed so that when the response is correct no shock ever arrives; only failure to respond results in shock. This second method of teaching is in some ways the most effective one. An animal once trained in this way to avoid shock will continue responding for long periods without any interference from the experimenter, whereas with other forms of teaching the reward must continue to be given.

This experimental result is thoroughly in accordance with common sense. Of course we too will do things to avoid unpleasant consequences, from crossing the street to dodge a bore, to paying income tax to avoid prosecution. It requires an effort to stand outside ourselves and ask whether this behaviour is understandable in terms of abstract principles such as the Law of Effect. Yet if we make this effort there is no doubt of the answer: avoidance learning does not fit in with the theory we discussed in the last chapter. Since the unpleasant state never arrives, ending it cannot act as a reward, and the marathon performances of animals trained by avoidance of punishment are therefore unrewarded. This kind of behaviour is, for the Law of Effect, a difficulty of the same kind as those we discussed earlier, concerning learning without reward.

Like the earlier difficulties, this one is easily explained by Tolman's 'map-inside-the-head' theory. We just have to suppose that an animal, which has experienced shock after failing to respond, and experienced no shock when it acts correctly, builds up a kind of model of the real world inside the nervous system. In this model each action is followed by its consequences, just as in the case of maze-learning Tolman's theory supposed a model or map in which the various parts were connected precisely as the corresponding parts of the maze were. Building up the model, learning, does not, according to Tolman, depend on reward. But the action produced will be the one which secures the consequences the animal most wants: and so he will respond in order to avoid shock even though he never gets a shock to remind him of the consequences of failure.

This kind of interpretation fits in nicely with common sense. All the same, in some places it comes close to assuming what we want to explain: one can understand the working model of the outside world built up in the nervous system, but this theory gives

77

no explanation of the way in which a desirable part of the model modifies action. Furthermore, when the case of avoidance learning first began to attract attention in the late Thirties, it had not yet become obvious that learning and performance should be kept separate and that learning as opposed to performance could be at full strength with only a moderate amount of reward. As we saw in the last chapter, these modifications of the Law of Effect are now commonly made for other reasons. But until they were, it seemed to many people as though any change towards Tolman's theory would undermine the value of the Law of Effect, and reduce us to the state of saying merely 'the animal does this because we would do the same in his place'. Consequently Tolman's theory was not generally acceptable and attempts were made to explain avoidance learning without departing from the Law of Effect.

One of the most successful attempts is the introduction of the concept of 'anxiety', and other 'secondary drives'. As we have said, an animal is usually said to be acted on by a 'drive' when it is restless and varied in its activity, and this restlessness can only be brought to an end by treating the animal in a particular way – giving it food if the drive is hunger, or water if it is thirsty. Now painful stimulation does arouse an animal just as hunger or thirst do. If a rat gets an electric shock, one sees a marked reaction in the form of sudden movements and bodily changes of the kind which we have previously mentioned as appearing in emotional states. Now this bodily response to pain appears also when any stimuli are present which previously accompanied the pain. If a dog has been treated cruelly, it may cringe at the sight of the room where the incident happened or of the person who was there. The notion of the 'secondary drive' is that this response which was once given to pain and now appears in the absence of pain is still a drive just as hunger and thirst are. But unlike hunger and thirst the secondary drive is satisfied by rewards which depend on the history of the particular animal. The reward is the removal of the stimuli which now control the emotional response, and this may well be different in different animals, depending on the circumstances in which they were originally hurt. In the case of avoidance learning, an animal which makes the correct response changes the situation from one in which he has been shocked (being in a certain place under certain conditions and having made no response), to one in which he has not (having made the avoidance response) and so reduces the secondary drive. The reward is not an obvious one, but it is a reduction in drive just as feeding a hungry animal is. In ordinary language, being in the cage where it was shocked makes the rat anxious or nervous, and raising its leg puts its mind at rest because it has never been shocked with its paw in the air. Although this language has some of the snags we mentioned in the first chapter, it does no harm so long as we remember how the word 'anxiety' is defined: and many people have in fact used that word to refer to the detached pain-response appearing to previously neutral stimuli.

This kind of thinking does have the advantage over Tolman's theory, that it gives some reason for the appearance of action as well as describing the way the animal learns the situation. In addition, the use of anxiety to explain avoidance learning keeps the Law of Effect intact, since the apparently unrewarded actions are now thought of as anxiety-reducing. The reader may by this stage be tempted to think of analogies in the human case, and it might be quite a useful exercise to let him do so: always remembering to distinguish clearly those features of human anxiety which are not really parallel to the animal experiments. But before we go on to analogies that have been put forward, particularly by O. H. Mowrer who was a leading figure in the rise of the concept of anxiety, we must round off one last point about the Law of Effect.

The original problem of avoidance learning was that the learned response seemed to be unrewarded. The theory of anxiety removed this difficulty by saying that anxiety would appear as soon as the situation resembled one connected with shock, and that the correct response was therefore rewarded by reducing anxiety. But there is still a step unexplained. The theory supposes a connection between the situation and the response of anxiety. What rewards or reinforces that connection, so long as the animal responds correctly and no shock occurs?

There are two ways to answer this question: to say that there is no reward for that connection, or to try to find one. Mowrer himself took the first course. The core of the anxiety response is after all in the glands, pulse rate, blood flow and other similar functions of the body, and Skinner had already put forward the idea that the Law of Effect applies only to actions such as limb movements: emotional changes in the body could perhaps be passed over from one stimulus to another without reward in the way that Watson held to be true for all responses. Mowrer took a view similar to this attitude of Skinner's: emotional responses, such as anxiety, could be attached to a situation simply by occurring previously in that situation. Actions more on an external level, such as walking or raising a limb, require reward; and in avoidance situations the reduction of anxiety keeps such actions alive. But the anxiety itself is passed over from its original painful stimulus to some other quite neutral one, merely because the two stimuli were contiguous in time.

The more orthodox followers of Hull disliked this modified theory, with its introduction of two principles of learning rather than a single unitary one. So they suggested that the anxiety was attached to the situation by its own reduction, in a vicious circle type of mechanism. When a shock or any other painful stimulus is presented, it must end sooner or later. This end is a reward, and makes more probable the responses which have just occurred. One such response is anxiety, and thus the anxiety is attached to the situation indissolubly.

This theory runs very much counter to common sense: it is tantamount to saying that one will learn to bang one's head against a wall because it is such fun when one stops. Mowrer and his associates therefore designed an experiment to compare the two theories. The technique used was simply to have a short signal to which the animal had to learn to respond: and varying durations of shock for incorrect response. The longer the shock, the more distant the end of it was from the signal, and therefore the less reinforcement there should be for anxiety when the signal arrived. On the view of the rigid Law of Effect theorists, then, learning should be better for short shocks and worse for long ones. In fact the result of the experiment does not bear this out at all. So the best bet at the moment seems to be Mowrer's double view, that anxiety is aroused by a situation simply because pain has been met in it, without any need for this emotional response to be rewarded. External actions, however, still need reward and one such reward is reduction of anxiety.

## Human Parallels

Without committing oneself to any of the detailed theories of learning which we have mentioned, one can see that the experiments say something about the nature of punishment which is applicable even to men. If one does something because it is regularly rewarded, any break in the connection between action and reward is immediately noticeable. But if one does something to escape punishment, then one may fail to notice that the outer world has changed and that no punishment will result from inaction. How could one know, without trying and so risking punishment? A habit of going to a particular restaurant can quickly be broken if that restaurant is closed: but a habit of avoiding a particular restaurant will not be broken just because the proprietor improves his treatment of his guests. As long as we stay away from his restaurant we shall know nothing about it.

Punishment is therefore an attractive technique for producing a certain kind of behaviour when one cannot be sure of being personally present to keep the behaviour going. This may be why the technique appeals so much to people who want to keep human behaviour within social bounds, discourage crime, and so on. If one cannot be sure of visiting every action with its just consequences there is a good deal to be said for using punishment for wrong actions. Once people have been trained in this way, they will still refrain from stealing even though there is no policeman about. After all, there might be one around the corner. We shall see the weaknesses and disadvantages of this way of governing society in due course: but it is important to appreciate the strength of the argument for punishment.

Another point about the persistence of behaviour established by punishment, is that it lets us reconcile with biological principles a number of human actions which are apparently futile and mal-adaptive. Many perfectly normal people go through small rituals before going to sleep, such as arranging their clothes in a particular way or making certain bodily movements. Yet there is no apparent reward or biological advantage in such behaviour. Equally a man may be compelled to visit his business and worry about its concerns long after he has retired, and there seems so little point in this that one wonders why the behaviour appears, on any evolutionary theory. In more extreme cases, people may be neurotically disabled by, for instance, inability to go to certain places although there is no real danger in those places. Such anxieties are troublesome and hard to root out, in a way in which more positive emotions are not. The clinical theories of neurosis lay a great deal of stress upon anxiety for this reason. Human experience confirms the lesson from animal experiments that anxiety will keep behaviour going long after the punishment which produced the anxiety has stopped.

Why, nevertheless, does punishment sometimes fail so con-spicuously to work? One reason is obviously that the original connection between action and punishment must be established. An animal experiment, again one in which Mowrer was involved, showed this neatly. Rats were shown food and shocked if they touched it immediately. Provided they delayed a short time they could eat the food without shock. When the time really was short, the rats learned this trick. But beyond a certain length of delay the connection of shock and of eating was too tenuous for a rat's fairly small brain, and they failed to learn. They succumbed to the immediate temptation of the food, and accepted the shock when it ultimately arrived.

In the same way most people would agree that human beings will not respond well to punishment given in no apparent relation to their behaviour. Punishment which arrives at long intervals out of the blue may be resented, but it will not stop any activity which gains an immediate reward. The connection between the action and its consequences must be made extremely clear. Of course this is to some extent true even if one is giving rewards for doing right, rather than punishing for doing wrong, but there is an additional danger in the use of punishment when a person (or an animal) cannot clearly see what it is that leads to punishment. He may in that case turn against the whole situation: in human terms, he may leave home because people are always on at him and he can't see why. This danger is not so great when reward is used, because even if somebody is not quite clear what leads to reward and what does not, he will at least keep on trying. The novice skier may have great difficulty in deciding why he sometimes blissfully descends a slope in fine style and why he sometimes comes to grief at once; but if the pleasure of success is big enough he will keep on trying until he becomes skilled. If, on the other hand, he is learning to ski in order to avoid being placed in an inferior position compared to his friends, if his failures are greeted with cries of scorn and his successes are not great enough to give him any great reward, then he may well abandon the sport.

Obviously, therefore, the degree to which reward or punishment is used may decide whether learning is successful or not. An animal experiment which illustrates this point shows also that it matters what kind of task is involved. In this experiment the animal is shown two doors which are slightly different, and if it goes through the wrong door it is given a shock. If the difference in appearance between the doors is big enough, the speed of learning depends on the size of the shock. The more severe the punishment, the more rapidly the animal learns to avoid the wrong door. But this ceases to be so true if the similarity between the doors is greater: we then find that increasing the punishment only produces more rapid learning up to a certain strength of shock, and after that point learning actually becomes less rapid with even more severe punishment. There is therefore a best value for the punishment, with inferior learning for weaker or for stronger shocks. The more difficult it is to distinguish the two doors, the lower is the best value for the punishment. This result, the Yerkes-Dodson Law, will find an echo in the experience of many people. In easy situations a powerful motive will help us to perform more efficiently; but in a tricky and delicate task there is such a thing as being too anxious, and when the consequences of failure are serious we may become unable to make fine discriminations and manipulations.

Some people have been known to draw a further conclusion from the points we have just made. As we have seen it is difficult for a rat to learn the connection between a present action and a punishment given at some future time. In so far as human beings do so there must be some processes inside their brains which connect each action with its possible future consequences. Now when these consequences are punishing, the action will be avoided: but we have also seen that there is a danger in animal experiments that the animal will avoid not only a particular wrong response but also the whole situation which involves punishment. It might therefore follow that human beings would avoid not merely the actions which lead to punishment, but also the processes in the brain which attach anxiety to those actions. Thus anxiety could be reduced not merely by avoiding the action, but by doing away with the mechanism which attaches anxiety to that action. In ordinary terms, one may refrain from making love to somebody else's wife because when one imagines doing it there are worrying elements in the thought: but one can also avoid worry by not even thinking about it. Although this is indeed a way of avoiding anxiety, it is a dangerous one because it abolishes the mechanism for controlling present behaviour by future consequences. Therefore actions may appear whch satisfy immediate drives but are from a longer-term point of view unsatisfactory.

Those who are at all familiar with psycho-analytic views will recognize in this argument something very similar to the concept of repression, in which according to Freud the ego renders unconscious those wishes which are irreconcilable with the demands of the super-ego: making use to do so of the anxiety which they arouse. The coincidence, between the views of clinicians engaged in treating patients and animal experimenters working on avoidance learning, would be more striking if Freud's theory had not been widely known by the time avoidance learning became a problem. But in fact the explanations of experimental results obtained with punishment were devised by people who had read Freud. Furthermore this account of the way in which people may become unaware of their own real motives, is in many respects not superior to the psycho-analytic one. Neither view is very clear about the dividing-line between self-deception and neurosis, about the reasons for repression appearing in some people but not in others living under similar circumstances, about the factors which decide what actions will in fact appear when the ordinary control mechanism has broken down, and so on; and the behaviouristic view has no more direct evidence in its favour than the clinical one does, for it is based on rather indirect argument from the type of experiments we have described. Nevertheless, the account in experimental terms is more congenial to some people, and it does at least offer the hope of a connection between the laboratory and those who deal with human problems every day.

Punishment has, then, the weakness that when its connection with action is not completely clear, it may produce a revulsion from right as well as wrong actions. In addition there is some evidence for another weakness: punishment does not simply reverse the action of reward, and therefore when it is used to oppose some pleasant action it does not really root out that action but merely suppresses it. On the views we have been mentioning, reward serves to forge a link in the nervous system between a stimulus and response, to make a given action more probable in a particular situation. But punishment on these views does not weaken a stimulus-response link; rather it attaches anxiety to a situation and this in turn causes removal from the situation to be rewarding. So even if punishment temporarily causes an animal to avoid some action that has previously been rewarded, the tendency to the action is still present and may operate if the anxiety produced by punishment is relieved. An example is given by the following experiment.

A rat is placed in a box with a lever, and rewarded with food each time it presses the lever. A certain number of rewards will bring the animal to a state in which, even if no more reward is given, it will go on pressing the lever for quite a while; and one can count how many of these unrewarded actions will appear before the animal gives up. If, however, the rat is given a shock the rate of lever-pressing will drop sharply so that one appears to have cancelled the effect of reward by punishment. Yet the drop in the rate of lever-pressing is only temporary: as time passes without repetition of the punishment the lever-pressing becomes more frequent again. The total number of actions made by the animal after a given number of rewards will in fact be much the same whether punishment is given or not: all that happens is a short-lasting drop in the rate at which they appear. The punishment stops the wrong actions today, but more appear tomorrow to make up the deficit.

This experiment gives us a definite hint that the advantage of punishment, in that it does not need to be given once anxiety has been established, is not one to be pressed too far. If an action is avoided for fear of punishment, and the person concerned once realizes that there is no longer any risk attached to the act, then the avoidance may break down altogether. On an everyday level, one remembers instances of children brought up under harsh discipline whose moral training seems to vanish once they escape from their home. Social psychologists have in fact observed events in children's clubs which are changed from an autocratic to a more democratic form of organization, and have shown that the results are less often satisfactory than they are in clubs organized democratically from the start. But the major weakness of punishment appears in situations where several motives are in conflict, as they so often are in human beings, and to these we shall now turn.

## Conflict of Motives

If we give an animal food at a particular place, and then take the animal a little way away while it is still hungry, it will try to get back to the place where it was rewarded. The strength of its tendency to go back varies with the distance to which one removes it: the further away one takes it, the less it tries to return. This slight falling-off of the tendency to approach the food can be measured directly by the curious means of fitting a little harness on a rat, attaching the harness to a spring balance, and recording how hard the rat pulls in its efforts to get back to the place of reward. The spring-balance reads less the further away from food one goes. This weakening of the rat's responses may, in some circumstances, be explained as due to the difference between the stimuli associated with the feeding-place and the stimuli now present: whenever a test stimulus is applied which is different from one to which some response is attached, the response weakens as the difference between original and test-stimulus increases. If a certain tune makes me think of somebody, other tunes will do so only so far as they resemble the first, and the less the resemblance the fainter and more elusive the memory of the person.

In other experimental conditions the weakening of the attraction of food with distance can be put down to the longer and longer delay which is likely to intervene between starting to run from more distant points and getting the reward of food. Any delay between action and reward weakens learning, and equally learning is particularly rapid at the end of a maze where the reward is usually given. In familiar situations, then, the rat will pull less to get at food if he is at a point where pulling will only be rewarded after a long trip to the food.

Remembering this change of attractiveness of food with distance, one can put an animal down half-way between two places both containing food. In such a case the attraction to the two places is equal, and there will therefore be a conflict within the animal. The case recalls the old story of the ass starving to death between two piles of hay. But in fact asses do not behave like that. Quite rapidly they choose one of the rewards and then settle definitely on it. How are we to explain this?

The equal attractiveness of the two rewards only holds so long as the animal remains poised at a certain place. Any chance movement to either side will strengthen the tendency to go further towards the food which is now nearer, and correspondingly weaken the tendency to go to the further food. Even if no chance movement occurs, some fluctuation may overtake the attraction of one reward, and immediately the same thing will happen. Once the balance of attraction is upset, the animal is pulled firmly over to the closer goal. This follows from the relation of attractiveness to distance, and it is found experimentally that conflicts set up in this way by putting two rewards in opposition are very easily resolved.

So much, then, for conflicts between rewards. Now the effect of giving a rat a shock, and then removing the animal to a distance, is broadly similar to that of the corresponding treatment using a reward. That is, the further away the rat is taken, the less it tries to move from the place it is put down; but of course it tries to get further away from the shock rather than to approach, as it did when rewarded. This obvious difference is very important when one considers an animal placed between two spots which are both associated with punishment. As before, the tendency to run away from one place may cancel out the tendency to run from the other, so that the rat does not go either way. But this time any chance movement away from this point of balance does not become exaggerated and lead to a complete cessation of the conflict. Anything which brings the rat nearer one of the two alternatives automatically increases the strength of the tendency away from that alternative and back towards the point of in-decision midway between the two. An animal suffering a con-flict between two courses of action which are both pleasant is like a pebble on top of a mountain: the slightest disturbance will send it finally and irrevocably over to one side or the other. But an animal in whom there is a conflict between two unpleasant possi-bilities is like a pebble at the bottom of a valley: even if it climbs a little way up one side of the valley, it tends to drop back and to find itself back in the original situation. The results of experiment confirm this analysis. Whereas an animal forced to choose between two rewards rapidly makes up its mind, an animal who is trying to avoid two punishments hovers between them and the conflict is likely to last a long time.

There is, however, one other fact which should be obvious to most people from everyday experience. A rat placed half-way between two places both associated with shock will not stay motionless at that spot but will try to get away in a direction at right-angles to the line joining the two places. Only by putting an insuperable barrier all round the space in which the experiment is performed can the animal be kept in the conflict situation. This fact also is not surprising, when we think in terms of the conflict-ing tendencies inside the animal. Only movement at right-angles to the line joining the two spots can possibly take the rat away from either without bringing it nearer the other. Opposing one unpleasant alternative with another therefore not only means a lengthy conflict, but also means that both alternatives will be dodged unless special measures are taken to make this impossible.

We have considered the conflict of two rewards, and that of two punishments. There remains the third possibility of a conflict between a reward and a punishment, between appetite and fear. The effect of this type of conflict is particularly striking and im-portant, and to understand it we ought to emphasize first another fact about the changes in attraction and repulsion which take place with distance. It was said earlier that the tendency to run towards a place associated with reward dies away with increasing distance from the place. So it does; but the rate of decrease is quite small, and even at large distances there is still a detectable trend back towards the goal. With punishment the change with distance is much more marked; close to the danger spot the animal is very keen to get away, but once a little space has been put between them the tendency to go further is much less marked. This difference reflects the basic division between reward and punishment: in the former case the drive, the arousing and unpleasant state which starts behaviour directed at reducing it, is inside the animal. Wherever the rat goes its hunger or thirst is still with it and prompting a return to the place of reward. In the case of punishment, however, the drive is attached to a particular situation, and drops off as soon as that situation is left behind. It is therefore very reasonable that the effect of distance on the attractiveness of a reward should be less than the corresponding effect on the avoidance produced by a punishment.

But this simple and reasonable difference between reward and punishment has important consequences when a conflict arises between them. In terms of the experiments we have been considering, this will happen when a particular place has been associated both with shock and with food, in the experience of a particular animal. If the rat is now placed far away from the spot where these mingled experiences occurred, it will be under a strong tendency to return to that spot: for as we have said the effect of reward does not die away as rapidly as that of punishment. So the animal will come back towards the crucial place. But as it does so the tendency to keep away from the punishment will grow more rapidly than the attractiveness of the reward. At length there will come a point of balance where the two tendencies are equal, and any further approach to the place of reward will cause the tendency towards flight to exceed that towards approach: so that the animal will reverse its movement, and come ultimately to a halt at the point of balance. Thus the conflict between reward and punishment, like that between two punishments, leads to a prolonged hesitation at a place which has no particular attraction of its own but which happens to be a boundary between conflicting tendencies. Yet there is still a difference between this type of conflict and that of two punishments. An animal which has experienced shock and food at the same place needs no external force to keep it in the conflict situation. Movement away from the goal in any direction produces always a tendency back towards the point of balance, so that the distance from the goal remains constant. It is possible for the animal to move around the circle whose centre is the goal, but not in or out so long as all the forces at work remain the same. Even more than the conflict between two punishments, this kind of situation locks the animal in a hopeless dilemma.

To summarize, a conflict between two appetites is in animals rapidly resolved in favour of the stronger. If an animal is forced to choose between two unpleasant alternatives it hesitates a long time and will escape from the situation altogether if it is not kept in it by special means. But if one place is both attractive and dangerous it will produce a lasting conflict in which neither tendency is satisfied, and no special means are necessary to keep the animal in this conflict. These results can be shown with animals: but they were first suggested by Kurt Lewin, who worked with children. Anybody who has to do with the young knows how much more rapidly they can choose between two sweets rather than between the unpleasant alternatives of tidying up their toys or going without supper. In the latter case it is also astonishing how many third courses of action they may take up to escape from the conflict. Lastly, a box of chocolates which a child is forbidden to touch, or an interesting animal which just might bite, can form for a very long time the centre of a fascinated circling. The differences between the different kinds of conflict seem to be inherent in the very nature of reward and punishment. Although no doubt they only appear in full simplicity in animals, there are some signs of similar processes in adult human beings. We have already mentioned the tendency for a child controlled chiefly by punishment to leave home as soon as he is able: only the impossibility of escape will keep him in a situation where uncongenial actions are forced on him by fear of even worse consequences. The dangers of approach-avoidance conflicts are perhaps to be seen in those persons who display a perpetual fascination with some desire which they dare not satisfy because of the anxiety it arouses in them. Although they may refrain from the act itself, the conflict interferes seriously with their lives and as we shall see may be very damaging in other ways besides waste of time. So far as these principles of conflict go, it is clear that reward has great advantages over punishment for the control of behaviour. We may wish perhaps to ensure that a human being does something unpleasant, such as working for an examination or giving the biggest piece of pie to the visitors. If we try to produce the behaviour we wish by punishing every other kind we shall have to take great trouble to prevent evasions and dodging, and even when we have almost secured the result we want there will be fresh hesitation and resistance. But if we give rewards of one sort or another, perhaps in the subtle form of developing interest in the subjects learned for the examination, there will be no need to prevent evasion and the problem will be simply one of making the incentive strong enough.

On the other hand, we may wish to discourage somebody from doing something which is in itself attractive: say, banging their enemy's head against the pavement or running off with his wife. Trying to prevent this by punishment may succeed so far as the actual deed is concerned: but even a strong punishment will do no more than create a point of balance at which the act is contemplated without being either put in hand or neglected altogether. It is less corrosive of personality to oppose these unwanted desires with other rewards, so that the conflict is resolved and the fascination lost.

This amounts simply to a restatement of the familiar doctrine, dear to the hearts of advisers on personal problems, that love of doing good is better than fear of doing evil. But writers in women's magazines less frequently point out the fatal flaw in controlling behaviour by reward: a few failures to be rewarded weaken the action, whereas something done to avoid punishment will be done even though objectively there would have been no punishment for inaction on this particular occasion. The adult may still feel too guilty to go to the cinema on Sunday, even though the father who punished him for such self-indulgence is long since dead. Had his father bribed him with sweets to stay home it is doubtful if parental influence would last longer than the bag of sweets. In the case of this example, many people nowadays might say that the good achieved was not worth any cost in anxiety: but we must beware of supposing that reward and punishment are used only for minor matters of behaviour. In any organized human society the primary drives – hunger, thirst, sex, and so on – cannot be left to be satisfied simply at the convenience of each person regardless of that of others. As we saw in an earlier chapter, different societies differ very much in their methods of meeting these needs, but within each society there is a necessary degree of uniformity. One can have a workable society in which men rule their households like tyrants, or one in which women do so, or one in which men and women are equal partners. What would be difficult would be a culture in which the husband was liable to adhere to one of these types of conduct and the wife to another. Socially acquired patterns of behaviour therefore govern much of our lives; human nature does not automatically fall into the form regarded as normal in Western Europe but does so only with much training. Because of the tendency for rewarded behaviour to extinguish when the reward stops, we would expect a great deal of this social learning to be based on anxiety unless special steps were taken to provide some other foundation. There is indeed considerable evidence of anxiety amongst people trying to adjust themselves to a satisfactory life.

One other result from animal work may allow the reader to make some suggestive observations for himself about the extent to which anxiety plays a part in man. If we attach our spring-balance to an animal and measure his tendency to approach a reward or flee a punishment, we find that the latter tendency is reduced by alcohol much more than the former. As a result, one can solve the worst kind of conflict, in which the same place is associated both with reward and punishment; one produces the solution by giving alcohol, whereupon the avoidance tendency is weakened and the approach tendency wins. Now looking about one at parties one can see men showing types of behaviour which may be attractive but which are not usually shown when no alcohol has been taken—particularly sexual and aggressive behaviour. It seems quite possible that when alcohol has this effect on a particular kind of action, that action is normally held in check by anxiety.

## The Effects of Conflict

So far we have only considered the various kinds of conflict from the point of view of the ease with which each can be resolved: the conflict of rewards is the easiest, and that between reward and punishment associated with the same goal is the worst. But inability to break free from a conflict has other results besides waste of time. So long as an animal stays in the conflict situation, the drives concerned remain at a high level. Not only do the positive needs such as sex or hunger remain unsatisfied, but, in situations involving anxiety, that drive also remains high because the signs of danger continue to be present. The effect of a drive is, as we have often said, to make the animal restless and variable in its behaviour and a prolonged conflict must therefore disrupt any regular patterns of action. Moreover, the bodily response which we have called anxiety is originally one with the purpose of adapting the body to pain and stress. Digestion stops, the heart speeds up, and so on. This change in the normal rhythm of life is useful for emergencies, but if it persists too long it is likely to do physical damage. These harmful effects of conflict have been shown in animal experiments.

When Pavlov was conducting his work on conditioned reflexes, he noticed that his dogs became very disturbed by some of the methods of training. The typical example is that of a dog which was given food every time one shape appeared but given nothing when another shape was shown. If there was a detectable difference between the shapes the dog simply learnt to salivate to one and not to the other. But if the shapes were too similar the dog not merely failed to react appropriately: it became very agitated, lost all its repertoire of other learned actions, and behaved oddly even outside the experimental situation. This disorder of behaviour became known as 'experimental neurosis'.

The name is rather an unhappy one, because it implies that the dog is suffering from the same disorder as a human being who has a neurotic illness. This is not at all a necessary conclusion, and it is a pity to beg the question by calling the dog's behaviour 'neurotic'. All the same, it is obviously important that certain learning situations are too much for the dog, and a good deal of experimental work has been done since Pavlov's time to confirm and extend his findings. One odd fact emerged quite soon: it is necessary for the animal to be held still by some sort of harness if experimental neurosis is to be produced. Pavlov's dogs were all held in this way, to make sure that they were looking in the right direction when the various patterns were shown to them. If the animal was left free, it would wander away and do something quite different when the task of distinguishing one stimulus from another got too difficult. In that case, no abnormal excitement or interference with other learning came about. It is as though the animal is only disturbed by being kept in a situation which resembles that associated with food, and yet which repeatedly fails to produce the promised reward. Certainly it is not just being faced with a difficult task which is disturbing, but only being faced with a difficult and inescapable task.

Up to this point it is probably fair to say that investigators of experimental neurosis thought of it in a rather intellectual way; the stability of the animal's nervous system was considered to break down because it was asked to make too difficult a distinction. But when the importance of restraining the animal was realized, attention was turned towards motives. Masserman performed a famous series of experiments in which he produced experimental neurosis in cats, without restraining them with a harness, by manipulating conflicting motives. He used an approach-avoidance conflict, which, as we have already seen, is the worst kind. The animal is held in a balance between appetite and fear, and the conflict is not easily resolved. Masserman gave cats food when a certain signal was given, but also gave them a strong blast of air when they approached the food. (An air blast of this sort is greatly disliked by cats.) Before long this situation produced very abnormal behaviour in the cats, some refusing to eat altogether, some going through strange ritual movements, and so on. Presumably Masserman's technique had this result despite the absence of any difficult discrimination, or restraining harness for the animal, because the combined reward and punishment automatically kept the cat in the conflict situation.

The disorganized behaviour seen in experimental neurosis is no doubt to a great extent simply that which any painful situation would arouse. Some of the 'symptoms', such as antagonism to the experimenter and reluctance to enter the laboratory, are very rational responses which cannot be compared to the irrational behaviour of a human neurotic: who may be antagonistic to people he has never met before or reluctant to go to places which are perfectly safe. All the same, the conflict situations used by Masserman are different from those in which an animal simply associates some place with pain. The conflict keeps the animal's drive at a high level, and so one may get abnormalities which would not be present in an animal avoiding pain. In the latter case he simply keeps away from the danger, while in the former he continues restless and disorganized.

Besides disrupting behaviour in this way, a continual high level of anxiety may have had effects on the body. Rats have been kept for long periods under conditions in which food and water were at opposite ends of their cage, so that a choice between satisfying one motive or the other always had to be made. These conditions of life had no harmful effect, as we should expect from our earlier discussions. A conflict between two appetites is rapidly resolved.

But when the rats were kept in cages in which food or water could only be approached at the cost of receiving an unpleasant electric shock, a high proportion of the animals developed stomach ulcers. Considering the effect of anxiety on the activity of the stomach, and the fact that an approach-avoidance conflict will not allow the anxiety to be reduced by leaving the situation, this damage to the stomach is not surprising.

## General Conclusions

All these unpleasant consequences have been demonstrated only from conflicts which involve anxiety and therefore punishment. These hazards must therefore be borne in mind when we think of punishment on the human plane. Yet, as we have seen, some of the characteristics of punishment make it almost inevitable that it will continue to operate. In Chapter V we will see a way in which reward may be given some of the advantages of punishment, which may help us in trying to get human beings to behave in a sociable manner. But people will to a large extent encounter their own punishments, independently of any deliberate effort to give pain to wrong-doers, and the effects of punishment will therefore remain important.

One last point should be noted about anxiety and conflict. In this chapter there have deliberately been interspersed highly objective animal experiments and very everyday dogmatic statements about human behaviour. The latter are, of course, on quite a different plane as evidence, and it is not quite fair to say that they can be put forward confidently on the basis of the animal results. Foresight and intelligence, an account of which we will give in the next chapter, play a greater part in man; and it is not certain that reward and punishment have the same characteristics when controlling actions chosen after deliberate forethought as they do in animal behaviour. But the results of the animal experiments harmonize very well with traditional wisdom about human affairs. Now in the first chapter we took a sympathetic glance at the feelings of people who reject objective psychology on the grounds

that it degrades human beings: they may perhaps feel that it
will lead to a world like that pictured by George Orwell or Aldous
Huxley. But it is surely also possible that principles reached by
behaviouristic techniques should reinforce the intuitions of past
spiritual leaders, rather than conflict with them. In fact, if we
have any real belief in the validity of humane principles we must
surely expect this to be so. It is a far cry as yet from the animal
laboratory to the conduct of our lives, but at least the results of
work on punishment make it likely that there will ultimately be
a connection.

# 4

# Reasoning in the White Rat

Any science tends to have occasional exchanges of views between theoretical opponents. One of the more entertaining exchanges in the history of psychology occurred in the late Thirties: and it may serve as an introduction to a chapter discussing the last and most serious criticism of the Law of Effect. This criticism is that correct action may often appear, at least in man, in entirely new situations. By thinking out a novel problem, a man may arrive at the answer although he has never tried any action at all: and as we shall see, the same is true of animals. While trial-and-error may be one form of learning, some people would argue therefore that it cannot be the only kind.

The particular controversy which we are going to start by considering, was begun by Tolman. His name should by now be familiar; he is the great supporter of the 'map-in-the-head' theory of learning. On this occasion he had thought up a situation in which his theory would predict one kind of behaviour while Hull would predict another. Tolman's idea was to teach rats to run along a path to food, and measure how fast they were running at the end of learning. He then proposed to put each rat directly into the food-box without letting it go through the rest of the path on the way: and he would then give the animal a shock in the food-box and put it back at the beginning of the path. He argued that since the beginning of the path had never been associated with shock, the rats should, according to the Law of Effect, simply start running as they had been trained to do. But on his own theory the result would be quite different. The map inside each rat's head would no longer indicate simply food at the end of the path, but would rather bear some equivalent of the statement 'here be electric shock'. So if the rats ran to the food-box at all they ought to do so in a rather slow and doubtful fashion, and the change in behaviour should be detectable. On Tolman's theory the rats should run slowly, while on his interpretation of Hull's theory they should run just as fast as they did before the shock was given.

The surprising feature of Tolman's paper was that he had performed the experiment: and got the result which he had *not* expected. Shock given in the food-box did not slow down the rats when they were placed back at the start of the path. It is not usual to find people testing their own theory by a method which turns out to disprove it, and, quite apart from the humour of the situation, Tolman's paper shows how far psychology had advanced scientifically since the days of the controversies about introspection which we mentioned in the first chapter. Not to be outdone in courtesy a supporter of Hull, named N. E. Miller, promptly published a repetition of Tolman's experiment with certain alterations, which had the effect of making the experiment produce the result Tolman had expected. So, roughly, speaking each side in the argument provided data corresponding to the other's views!

But Miller had a reason for altering Tolman's technique, and in his paper he explained this reason. To state his view, an animal is aware not only of the outside world but also of its own actions. As a result, if a series of actions (say, running through the various alleys of a maze) is followed by reward, there is by the Law of Effect a tendency for each action in the series to produce the next action even though the outside situation is not appropriate. Furthermore, any action includes not only large, obvious, and slow movements, but also hidden ones which may be much faster: when a rat looks at a particular path in a maze, some part of its brain must respond to the peculiar features of that path and this response like any other can be joined into a series built up by reward. So a fully trained rat will, when looking at the start of a maze, perform a series of very minor responses (perhaps purely within its brain) which correspond to the series of actions involved in running through the maze. The end of this series will be a response which is part of the whole complex action of taking the reward: so if food is the reward we might expect the trained rat to lick its lips when it sees the start of the maze, or even merely to have some activity in a part of its brain which normally responds to food.

This argument had been put forward previously by Hull, and he called the last of the minor responses, the lip-licking or brain activity, the 'fractional anticipatory goal response'. Understandably most people find this a mouthful, and the concept is usually talked about as $r_g$. Applying these ideas to Tolman's experiment, Miller argued that the rat at the beginning of the path ought to be showing the $r_g$ corresponding to the food-box: but since shock had been given in the food-box, $r_g$ should give rise to a response to shock. Therefore even at the start of the path the rat should show responses to shock and therefore be reluctant to run.

On this argument, the slowing-down is mediated by $r_g$, and it is therefore essential that this response should be the same when the rat is shocked as it was when the animal was fed during training. Otherwise there will be nothing to connect the shock with the pathway leading to food. This means that the food-box must be very distinctive, so that it produces a suitable $r_g$. In everyday language, the rat has to notice the food-box and be quite clear that the shock is being given in the same place that lies at the end of the path. So Miller made the food-box in the form of a sharp bend, which meant that the rat had to eat with its head and shoulders turned out of line with its body: and as we have already said his animals showed reluctance to run towards the food-box after they had been shocked in it.

This behaviour on the part of the rat is rather endearingly human. A man placed in the same situation would 'put two and two together'. He would say to himself: 'If I run down this path, I shall get to the food-box. But that's where I was shocked, so I'd better go carefully.' The resulting actions would be sensible, and quite unlike the undirected variety of actions usually called trial and error. Miller's explanation of the rat's success is also very like the sort of introspective account a man might give of the same problem. He might say that seeing the path made him think of the food-box, but then that reminded him of shock, and this discouraged him from acting. If we can say that Miller's $r_g$ corresponds to 'thinking about the food-box', this is the same process that is supposed to go on in the rat. Of course, it is not legitimate to translate an $r_g$ simply into a thought, with all the overtones and associations that arise in our minds when we use a word like 'thought'. But there do seem to be some similarities in the two ideas. The fact that it is necessary to suppose something like the $r_g$ to explain the rat's behaviour means that we need not be surprised to find our own actions rather more complex than earlier chapters have assumed animal behaviour to be. The question is, how far must some internal processes be supposed to go on inside animals, symbolizing the flow of events in the outer world and thus corresponding even crudely to our own forethought and reasoning? From Watson's time until almost the present day, this has been a matter for debate. Let us have a look at some of the evidence.

## The Insight of Apes

While Watson was introducing the conditioned reflex into psychology, a German psychologist was marooned on the Canary Islands by the outbreak of the 1914–18 war. His name was Köhler, and he made use of his time to study the behaviour of apes. In particular he watched how they solved strange problems never met before; and his work has formed the foundation of a whole area of research ever since.

To begin with, there are some new situations which apes cannot handle. If in order to get food they have to unwrap a rope from a bar round which it is twisted, they pull at the rope in a random and unintelligent fashion. Equally even an animal which has practised reaching through the bars of its cage with a stick and pulling in food, will not usually break a branch off a tree to substitute for a stick when the experimenter puts food just out of reach but provides no stick. They do not 'see' the solution of the problem in such cases. But in other situations where the main features of the difficulty are laid out more conspicuously, the ape will produce some quite new and yet correct action. For instance, if a banana is hanging from the ceiling and is too high for the ape to reach, the animal may pick up a box and move it underneath the banana so that he can climb on it. If one box is not enough, he may pile up two. But, as far as can be made out, just this particular action has never happened before and so cannot have been built up by reward according to the Law of Effect. Something other than past reward makes the action appear. On the other hand, this kind of 'insightful' act is not simply one of the chance pieces of behaviour which are tried out by an animal during trial and error learning. If anything interferes with the action (say, a box falling off the pile) it is immediately repeated. In trial and error one action is not usually tried twice or more often in succession. Besides, the insightful act once successful is repeated whenever the appropriate situation arises: it does not simply become more probable, but is almost perfectly learned in one trial. In ordinary language, the ape knows that the boxes will get him to the banana even before he gets there, and after his success the action is perfectly learned because he understands the principle.

The view held by Köhler and his successors was that insight was achieved by a reorganization of the brain processes corresponding to the various features of the external situation. The whole arrangement, cage, bananas, boxes and all, was represented inside the ape by a pattern of events in the brain: and this pattern would force some of the nervous processes to go in a particular direction and so to solve the problem. An analogy might be the way in which a soap bubble is pulled into a round shape by the whole pattern of forces on the bubble. Any one part of the bubble is forced to take up the correct position to fit in with the others. In the same sort of way the gap between the cage-floor and the banana produces in the ape's brain a distorted pattern which is only brought into balance when the animal fills the gap with the boxes.

In support of this kind of theory one could cite experiments on making problems difficult for the ape to solve. For instance, an animal which was not used to reaching for food with a stick would not use one, even when it was provided, if the stick was laid crosswise to the line of sight rather than pointing at the food. It was easier for the animal to learn to use the stick if it was already directed towards the right place. One could think of this effect as due to a change in the pattern of forces in the brain: a stick pointing towards the food gave a pattern which forced a solution just as a soap-bubble is forced into a round shape. A stick laid crosswise spoiled the pattern just as a pin stuck through the soap-film might do.

On such a view a pattern which is spoiled for a time may jump into shape suddenly for some accidental reason. It is indeed true that an ape will sometimes, after brooding over a problem, suddenly hit on the solution with great enthusiasm. One classic incident was recorded by Köhler and is now almost too well known: but it deserves to be repeated. An ape had been given two short sticks and was tempted with some food lying at a distance too great to reach with either stick. After attempts to make the impossible stretch, the animal abandoned the food and began to play with the sticks. By accident one stick got pushed into a hole in the end of the other, thus making one long stick. The ape leapt up, stopped playing, and going back to the food, pulled it in with the now long stick. This sudden recognition of a solution will bring back familiar memories to human beings who have wrestled with problems: even such simple ones as crossword puzzles. After a period of bafflement the answer comes with a bang, perhaps because of some chance remark by a friend, or a memory called up by some picture. From then on the answer to the puzzle seems obvious and it is almost unbelievable that one had not recognized it earlier.

So far as behaviour goes, the apes show all the features of such an intellectual achievement: the correct action appears suddenly without any clumsy trial and error, and it is repeated in similar situations as though the principle was now obvious to the animal. Insight is not a quality peculiar to man, and it must be recognized as a category of behaviour very different from the slow perfecting of actions learned by trial and error. This does not necessarily mean that the basic explanation of the behaviour is different in the two cases. In another field of science, the force which causes an apple to fall to earth has been identified as that which holds the planets in their orbits. A common cause may lie behind two very different effects. But we must still distinguish the effects, and not get confused between apples and planets. Equally, insightful behaviour is very different from that which appears in a puzzle box and which we described in Chapter 2.

## Problem Solving by Rats

Apes are animals closely related to ourselves, and if they show insight, that need not mean that this form of behaviour is a basic and widespread one. It might simply be some peculiarity of our branch of the animal family. In addition, apes are more difficult to breed and bring up under controlled conditions than smaller and shorter-lived animals are. So there was and indeed is still, a great deal of interest in the study of insight in rats. Any experiment showing it would carry the implication that this category of behaviour was an important one for animals in general. If insight does need some other principle to explain it, in addition to those used for trial-and-error learning, that principle would need to take equal rank with those we have already discussed.

It will by now be no surprise to find that Tolman's name is associated with one of the classic demonstrations of processes other than trial and error in the rat. The technique used in this case was to teach the animal a maze in which there were three ways of getting to the goal. One way was short and direct, and another very long and roundabout. The third was of intermediate length, and it joined the short one a little way before the goal. Now a rat soon learns in a maze of this type to take the shortest possible route: he is no more disposed to waste energy than we are. This is, of course, easily explained by the more rapid reward which the choice of the short path receives. If we now block the shortest path the rat will come back from the block to the start of the maze, and can there choose either the medium or the long path. If the block is beyond the junction of the two shorter paths, however, choosing the medium path will not be successful. Yet choosing that path has in the past been rewarded more rapidly than choosing the long path has. So a simple Law of Effect theory would predict that the medium length path would be chosen – whereas if the animal possesses insight, if there is a pattern of events in its brain which parallels the structure of the maze, it will know that the medium path is also blocked: and it will choose the long path.

In fact the long path is indeed the one chosen. This experiment has been repeated a number of times with various modifications, some of which have misled the rat so that it does not succeed in choosing the unblocked but long path. But there are results in which the original finding has been repeated under conditions which allow no simple explanation on the lines of the Law of Effect. So we have to conclude that the rat will produce a response when appropriate even though it is not the one most rewarded: he possesses 'insight' into the arrangement of the alleys of the maze.

Although this experiment shows that the animal has achieved a state similar, so far as behaviour goes, to that of a man who understands some problem, it does not give us anything corresponding to the puzzled thought and sudden illumination which may precede the first solving of a human problem. Köhler's apes did show behaviour which reminds one of these stages of thought, and the word 'insight' was used to refer to the moment of success as well as to the state of an animal which had succeeded. Everybody would agree, of course, that the flash of achievement, in which a new solution is found, must be based on past experience.

The ape which suddenly solved the problem of reaching with two short sticks had had previous familiarity with the use of a single stick, and it also had the chance experience of seeing the two sticks joined together. Without these experiences the problem would never have been solved: but the novelty consisted in combining the separate experiences into a new whole. In the same way a human mathematician does not solve a problem completely out of the blue, but builds his new solution on a knowledge of existing techniques. The description of insight as a restructuring of the perceptual pattern, given by Köhler's followers, enshrines this distinction between the past and the present achievement. All the elements necessary for solving the problem may be present, but they have to be recombined. Can one show this phenomenon in rats?

About 1930, a series of experiments were carried out by Maier, which showed that separate experiences could indeed be put together. For instance, a table might be divided into two parts, A and B, divided by a partition through which a rat can see but not walk. A can be reached from the ground but B cannot. An animal is allowed to explore the room in which the table stands, including climbing up to A. Then a set of bridges are fitted up in the room, starting from B and ending at a point which can be reached from the floor of the room. The rat is allowed to climb up from the floor, explore the bridges, and so find his way to B. At this stage he knows that one can reach A from the floor, and that one can also reach B from a different part of the floor: the two experiences having been separately acquired. He is then put at A with food visible at B.

In order to reach the food the rat must do something he has never done before, namely, climb down from A and then up from the floor to the bridges which will lead him to B. This is a new combination of the old experiences: and it is in fact what the animal does. Of course this one experiment, particularly as we have described it, is not enough to prove that rats show a true ability to solve new problems. The solution might, for example, have been reached by chance. But once again there are various modifications of the experiment which rule out simpler explanations: one can for instance offer the rat a choice of two or more paths so that one knows the odds against a correct choice by chance, and show that the rat does nevertheless choose correctly more often than chance would allow.

So we have to conclude that even in rats not all actions appear merely because they have been rewarded in the past. Some appear because they will be rewarded in the future: if they were human actions, we would say that the person concerned 'foresaw' that a certain way of behaving would bring reward in this new situation, and so decided upon it even though he had not acted in that way previously. This kind of conscious rational action seems at the furthest remove from the mechanical selection of some acts out of a medley of chance ones, by the Law of Effect. Yet the findings are objective and experimental, rather than merely introspective reports that a certain form of behaviour is associated with conscious purpose. We cannot deny that behaviour of this sort, never previously rewarded, occurs. The question is whether it can be reconciled with the fairly simple mechanisms we have described already.

## Insight and Internal Responses

At the beginning of this chapter we considered Miller's account of the behaviour of rats entering a path at the far end of which they had been shocked. In that account the sight of the beginning of the path started a series of events within the rat's brain; and this series was made up of the processes which would have happened in the brain had the rat been really and physically running along the path. At the end of the series there came the response, inside the brain, which would normally be given to shock: and so the rat was less willing to enter the path. An explanation like this one can be given for experiments of the type performed by Maier. We can suppose that when an animal is in some new situation it will run off internally each of the learned series of actions which are possible to it. If one of these series finishes with an action which forms the start of some other, separately learned, series, that too will be run off. And if this second series ends in a consummatory act such as taking food when hungry, the whole chain formed by the two series of responses will tend to appear in real action as well as in the fractional unobservable form.

For example, suppose a rat is taught to run from place X to place B to find food when hungry. It could also be taught, when satisfied with food but thirsty, to run from A either to X or Y, water being put at both places. Now if it is made hungry again and put at A, it should have an equal slight tendency to go either to Y or to X, and both these actions are tried out internally. The brain-process corresponding to Y is irrelevant to a hungry animal: so also is that corresponding to X, but the latter does start a fresh series of brain-processes which end up with one corresponding to food. This we called earlier $r_g$, the fractional anticipatory goal response. When this response occurs in a hungry animal, the chain of nervous events leading to it is strengthened and translated into action: so the rat runs from A to X and then to B, which is a sequence never previously performed.*

On this view, new problems are solved by an internal process of trial and error, very similar to the ordinary kind, but unobserved because it happens within the nervous system. The combination of separate past experiences comes about through the common elements at the end of one series of actions and the beginning of another. In complicated situations there may well be a long delay before the right combination occurs, because there may be many courses of action to try out internally, and the situation may tend to emphasize the wrong starting series and to conceal the correct one. For instance, in experiments in which an animal sees food through a wire mesh it is particularly difficult to reach any solution which involves walking *away* from the food.

* This explanation is not the only one which can be produced from Hull's theory, nor is it the one most common in text-books. It is, however, the one put forward by Hull himself. For a discussion of alternatives, see the Appendix.

The difficult problems mentioned earlier, of breaking a branch off a tree to act as a reaching stick, or of using a stick placed across the line of sight, could be regarded as hard for this kind of reason. The first actions involved in breaking off a branch are rather unlikely ones in a problem of getting food, and a stick is more likely to be associated with motion of objects lying along its own length. Most puzzles which amuse and baffle human beings have a similar element. When a puzzle requires one to ferry a certain number of missionaries over a river without ever allowing them to be outnumbered by their cannibal boatmen, the difficult first step is likely to be the ferrying over not of any missionaries, but of some of the cannibals: which is not an action immediately suggested by the problem. When a puzzle requires the measuring out of a certain quantity of milk from one jar with the aid of two other jars of quite different capacity, it is peculiarly difficult to find a solution which involves pouring some of the milk back into the original jar. Detective story writers are well aware of this tendency for a strong and obvious line, of internal trial and error, to exclude other possibilities: so that at one time it was safe for the sophisticated reader to assume that the 'obvious' suspect was not the criminal. The author would combine honesty with surprise by providing all the evidence necessary to identify one character in the book as guilty, but effectively stop the reader from completing the chain of reasoning by strongly suggesting some other incomplete chain pointing to another character. Nowdays the author may sometimes assume sophistication in the reader and conceal the criminal by pointing suspicion at him: but psychologically this is still making him the person least likely to arouse internal trial and error. A brief demonstration of the importance of misdirection can be given by asking somebody for the meaning of the sentences 'Pas de Lieu rhône que nous' and 'Caesar adsum jam forte'. So long as he regards them as French and Latin he is likely to struggle unavailingly and it is only when he reads them aloud and listens to them simply as sounds making English sentences that he will recognize their very simple meaning.

In any novel situation, then, the first responses to be tried out internally will not be completely random. There are always some features of a problem which are familiar, and so will arouse attempted solutions of the same type as those used in earlier problems with the same features. If these lines of solution can be combined with other past experiences so as to produce an answer to the current problem, the correct action will appear immediately. If on the other hand the first arising courses of action are unable to lead to success, there will be a long delay followed by a sudden solution when the first suggestions die away from lack of reinforcement and are replaced by others. Animals (and people) will of course differ not only in the number of experiences they have available for trial but also in the speed and certainty with which they will reject unsuitable lines of attack. There is such a thing as the individual who is consistently good at dealing with novel situations.

Now, how does this explanation in terms of internal trial and error, fit in with the one in terms of 'insight'? There is a lot in common between the two: both suppose in the brain a set of events corresponding to the set of real events in the outer world, both suppose that the internal processes can be combined in various patterns, and both suppose that success is achieved when they are combined in the particular pattern which corresponds to the solution of the problem. Once that pattern is achieved the animal will suddenly produce a complete, though new, action and repeat it if it is hindered or if a similar situation reappears. But there are some differences between the theory which stems from Köhler and Tolman and that which comes from Hull, and these have been debated for the last twenty years. As experimental evidence has built up, there has been more and more agreement; and now the differences have really vanished. It is worth considering briefly what they were, before going on to mention the points which the new combined view still leaves uncertain. Firstly, the analogy with physical processes like blowing soap-bubbles puts much more importance on the actual structure of the brain than does a theory of combining previously learned responses. The latter view seems to make the difficulty of solving certain problems merely a question of having had the wrong experiences, while the other theory suggests that some problems are difficult because they require patterns that the brain cannot easily form. Now one must admit that hereditary as well as acquired difficulties may appear in problem solution: a guinea-pig is less likely than a ferret to hit on a solution which involves biting the experimenter. (This experiment does not seem to have been tried, but the fact can perhaps be accepted nevertheless!) The Hullian theory therefore has been forced to include the idea that different solutions may differ in probability innately as well as through experience. On the other hand, research on the nature of nervous activity has not supported very well the original suggestion of Köhler and his associates about the particular way in which patterns form in the brain. So it is perhaps a good thing to be rather agnostic about this, as the Hullians are, and not to try and explain why one solution is more difficult until we know more about the workings of the nervous system.

A second point of difference concerns the nature of the internal processes. On a simple Hullian view, they are small parts of responses of the animal, and therefore correspond only to real actions and not to any other feature of the outer world. On the other theory, and especially perhaps on Tolman's version of it, they may correspond to events in the outer world which are only observed by the animal. To Tolman the rat may have inside his head a map of a maze, but not a string of muscle twitches like those he would make running through it. The distinction is shown up by the experiment of Maier's which we described earlier. A rat which has gone from the floor to A and from the floor to B will go from A to the floor and so to B: that is, it combines its knowledge of the two routes but its actions may be the opposite of those produced in the earlier experience. Because of this type of experiment the supporters of Hull would admit that the internal responses required by their theory need be no more than the changes in the brain usually produced by outside stimulation. They should still perhaps be called responses to make it clear that they are supposed to be physical events and not sensations or ideas in the consciousness of the animal: but it is generally agreed that they are not confined to symbolizing the animal's own movements but may also stand for events altogether separate from him.

The third and last of the differences between Tolman and Hull is perhaps the most important. By the Law of Effect the separate experiences, which were combined to solve a new problem, should each have been followed by reward. Only by reward can the internal responses be learned and so be available for recombining. On Tolman's theory, however, the map inside the head is built up without reward. Here again the Maier experiment mentioned earlier shows the sort of evidence which is relevant. Some of the experience used in solving the problem was given simply by letting the rat explore, without rewarding it in any very noticeable way. Now as we saw in Chapter II, Hull had for rather similar reasons said that very small rewards would produce as much learning as large ones would: but that increasing the motivation by increasing the drive or the reward would produce a greater tendency to make use of learning. Performance depends on the amount of reward, learning does not. This goes a long way towards explaining how an animal can make use in solving problems, of experiences which were apparently unrewarded: but it is often difficult to see even a very slight reward in such cases. What reward, for example, followed when Köhler's ape joined the two sticks together? Yet that experience was combined with others in order to solve the problem of getting food from outside the cage. There must therefore have been strong 'internal responses', despite the absence of apparent reward.

Spence, one of the most eminent supporters of Hull, has recently modified the theory even further. On this revised view the importance of reward is merely that one of the internal responses corresponds to it: when food is given at the end of a path the series of internal responses corresponding to the path ends up with $r_g$, the anticipatory goal response of food. If now during a process of internal trial and error the $r_g$ occurs, the motivation of the animal rises so highly that it begins to make real actions and so to carry out the behaviour which was formerly only symbolized. Internal responses other than the $r_g$ do not have this effect, and this is why reward must at some point have been given if the animal is to be made to perform. But reward does not, on Spence's view, fix actions permanently in the animal's repertoire as the simple Law of Effect held. Like Tolman, Spence now holds that learning may need no reward at all, but that performance will only appear if some reward is to be gained by it.

This view can be put in human terms something like this. Suppose I find a restaurant by taking a certain route from Piccadilly Circus, and get well fed there. My resulting tendency to take that route again when hungry shows the simple Law of Effect. But if I now find a route from Liverpool Street to Piccadilly Circus, it is not necessary to give me some food in the Circus to ensure that in future I will be able to go from Liverpool Street to the restaurant. Hull therefore modified the Law of Effect so that only very slight reward would explain my learning of the second part of the route – perhaps my pride in geographical exploration, or the pleasant associations of Piccadilly Circus. Spence modified the Law even more by saying that both parts of the route were learned without needing reward, but were performed only because when I think about them I also think of the restaurant.

Another way of restating Spence's view is to remember the account of anxiety given in the last chapter. If a stimulus has in the past been present when pain occurred, that stimulus now calls forth the response to pain, and so the animal avoids the stimulus. On Spence's view, a stimulus which is associated with reward calls forth the response to reward, and so the animal seeks the stimulus. Anxiety, as we saw, is attached to a situation simply by occurring in that situation. It then acts as a factor controlling action. Equally the $r_g$ or other internal responses are regarded as attached to a situation purely by occurring in that situation: and then the $r_g$ controls action.

With these alterations and modifications there no longer seem to be any serious differences between the idea of problem-solving as achieved by internal trial and error and that of insight. Although some people may prefer one language and some the other, the important thing is that everyone agrees that animal behaviour can only be explained by supposing processes in the brain which stand for or symbolize the outside world and which can be recombined to produce solutions to novel problems. One question which immediately strikes one is, how far is human thought more than this? No answer can be given. Obviously any human being carries this process much further than any animal. He has a vastly greater array of 'internal responses' at his disposal, and therefore can recombine them in a bewildering variety of ways. And it is conceivable that there may be in our thinking some further function which is really of a different kind from that of animals, rather than the same kind in enormously greater quantity. But if there is such a further function, nobody has as yet succeeded in describing it in ways which can be made subject to experiment. Every attempt which has been made to state some general principle of thought which is never shown by animals has ended in failure. This should not lead us to despise thought: rather we ought to look on animals with a new respect, as creatures far more complex than the simple, almost clockwork, models of Watson and the early Law of Effect. Furthermore even though the principles of animal and human problem-solving may be the same, this does not mean that their achievements are of equal value. The principle which upholds the dome of St Paul's cathedral is the same as that which preserves a child's arch of bricks built over a toy railway line. Recognition of the principle as the same is a vital step towards building domes, but of course a cathedral is neither technically nor spiritually 'nothing but' a child's toy. Equally there is a difference in scale and value, though perhaps none in principle, between human reasoning and that of the white rat.

## Some Remaining Uncertainties

Although insightful behaviour requires the general kind of mechanism we have discussed, it does not specify very exactly what the rules are which govern the internal responses. A simple rule would be that they obeyed exactly the same principles as ordinary observable responses of the kind studied in trial and error experiments. But this principle will not do. A British psychologist, Deutsch, has pointed out that if we use this simple rule then an internal response will be reinforced by any reward which comes along immediately afterwards. So if the animal happens to have an $r_g$ for eating just before it is given water that should strengthen the internal response for eating. Next time it is hungry it ought to go rushing towards the place where it satisfied its thirst! In fact if an $r_g$ can be strengthened by *any* reward we cannot use it to explain why an animal seeks out the place associated with the *right* kind of reward. A good guess at a principle which will get round this difficulty is, that an animal only learns to make a particular internal response in a certain situation if the corresponding external action occurs: so only food can reinforce the $r_g$ corresponding to eating, and only water the $r_g$ corresponding to drinking. But since the $r_g$ by its nature cannot be observed, we cannot be sure yet if this is true.

A similar difficulty is shown up by the following experiment. Suppose we run a hungry rat in a maze which has two possible paths, which look different but both have food at the end of them. Part of the way down one path we put some water; and when the rat has run through the maze a number of times we make it thirsty and see whether or not it goes to the water. One might conceivably argue that if the water is a long way down its path, almost at the food, the $r_g$ corresponding to water would be heavily rewarded and so the rat would learn the whereabouts of water very well. When thirsty, it should go down that path and not down the other. But actually it does so more easily if the water was placed near the beginning of the path, a long way before the food is reached. Why is this a particularly good situation for building up the correct $r_g$?

One possible explanation is again due to Deutsch. The brain process, whatever it may be, which symbolizes food, is the only one which is the same for both paths. The closer the water is to the food, the more it therefore tends to be linked with both paths rather than simply with its own surroundings. Separating the water from the food prevents the confusion between the two paths.

Yet a third difficulty can be illustrated by another experiment. In this case a rat has the choice of two paths. Either of them will lead to a box in which the rat will be kept for a short time: and at the end of that time he has an even chance of being rewarded, no matter which path he takes. The box in which he is kept is some-times black and sometimes white, again no matter which path he takes. The only difference between the paths, in fact, is that on one side the box is always white when the rat is going to be rewarded and black when he is not; while if he takes the other path the colour of the box has nothing to do with the chance of reward. According to any principle we have mentioned so far, the rat ought not to prefer one path to the other. But in fact he chooses the one which will keep him in suspense for the least time, that is, the one where the colour of the box is a sign of the coming reward.

Once again we can make a possible explanation. When the colour of the box tells the animal whether reward is coming, it becomes worth noticing, and so the rat is far more likely to make internal responses to the colour. When colour is unrelated to reward, observing responses are less likely and thus the chain of internal processes corresponding to the events between the choice of path and the taking of food will be weaker. But one cannot say that these particular explanations are as satisfactory as the general conception of symbolic internal processes is, and obviously many further experiments need to be done. They are now in progress in many places, and they involve such things as teaching animals with one drive and then testing them with another, varying the kinds of differences between the various paths of mazes, changing the level of drive, and so on. From all these studies we may get a more adequate idea of the factors which cause a particular feature of the world to be represented by an internal response with the animal's brain.

Yet the internal response itself remains unobserved. We have to infer its nature from behaviour, and this introduces a new and slightly discordant note into a science which was supposed to deal only with public data. Is it really legitimate to talk about the things which go on out of sight inside the animal? Of course this problem had appeared earlier in other forms, and the $r_g$ merely makes it acute. A drive, for example, is equally something about an animal which is not obvious to casual inspection. A hungry rat differs from a satiated one in its history and in what it will do in possible future circumstances, but the two animals can look very much the same. To find out which one of them possesses a drive one must ask the man who looks after their feeding which one has had food lately: or one must try giving each of them food every time some action is made, and see which animal learns to make that action. From these observations we can infer the presence of a drive. And yet most people would say that the drive is something inside the animal and not directly observable. We seem to be in danger of introducing something as private as any introspection into our science. To get out of this difficulty, some behaviourists denied that the drive was anything more than the set of observations we make to decide whether it is present. If we say 'the Jones family was not in church last Sunday' we mean that we did not see Mr Jones, Mrs Jones, nor their son, nor their daughter. We do not mean that there is some fifth thing, the family, which could have been in church although none of the four people were to be seen. Equally, so it was argued, we can only say that a rat has a hunger drive in the sense that we can make the kind of observations already mentioned. Unless those observations are made there is no drive, and one can translate any sentence containing the word 'drive' by a more complicated sentence containing the necessary observations. It is a convenient short label for a large array of data which is perfectly public and respectable.

This attitude found a good deal of moral support in the direction taken by physical concepts during the first half of this century. In physics a number of advances have been made by recognizing that certain questions, which seem to mean something, are not real questions because there is no possible way of finding an experimental answer to them. If we ask, for example, what the true velocity of the earth is, not the velocity around the sun, or the speed with which the earth is rushing away from a particular star, but the 'true' speed – there can be no answer. As soon as we make an actual measurement of velocity, we have to put in some frame of reference, and the result of the measurement is relative to that frame. So it is a waste of time to discuss any 'true' velocity independent of actual conceivable observations.

In a similar way, it is useless to talk about the position and velocity of an electron simultaneously, because any way of finding out one of these quantities automatically disturbs the other. Again one has to define one's concepts in terms of possible observations, and to avoid attaching any reality to something when there is no way of observing it.

These doctrines were taken over into psychology, and it was suggested that any concept used in the science of behaviour should be regarded simply as the sum of the observations defining it: it was an 'intervening variable' serving only the shorthand purpose already mentioned, but with no physical reality. In its extreme form this view would imply that it was pointless to look for any physiological element corresponding to a 'drive', or for that matter to an $r_g$. The study of the brain ought to go on independently of the study of behaviour, because nothing could be concluded about events in the nervous system simply by studying actions. Such a schism between two methods of studying human beings seems undesirable, but the problem is a real one. In the next chapter we shall stand back a little from experimental findings and consider various points of view about the proper way to deal with theoretical ideas as opposed to observed facts. The reason for doing so at this stage is that we have seen how the original simple generalization, that rewarded actions become more frequent, has had to be modified and extended. Learning may take place when no action does, and it is performance rather than learning which is affected by increase in reward. The avoidance of pain gives performance which persists for a long time, although neither reward nor punishment is given, so that we have to postulate an acquired drive within the animal. And in this chapter we have seen that sometimes animals will make quite new actions in a way which presupposes some complex events going on inside the brain and symbolizing the pattern of the outside world. The study of behaviour has forced us to realize that even for animals a simple rule like the Law of Effect will not wholly serve. Our theories must be more complicated, and so we ought now to examine the ways in which more complex theories can be built.

# 5

# Fact and Theory

Many people, even among those who go no further in mathematics, meet the geometrical theorems of Euclid at school. These theorems are a set of proofs of the properties of common figures: for example, of the fact that the angles of any triangle add up to two right angles. Such facts are proved by logical deduction from a few definitions and postulates which are assumed to be true: for example, that parallel lines never meet. Throughout the argument, words are used only with meanings which they have clearly been defined to possess, and nothing is assumed without the assumption being written out fully so that the reader can judge its reasonableness for himself. The result is a style of argument which is austere and rigorous to such an extent that it has fascinated men throughout the thousands of years that the books have existed. Nothing could be further from psychological theories as usually understood: from, for instance, the works of Freud or William James. Even Watson's books are quite clearly of another breed than Euclid's; they persuade in a way which leaves the reader able to disagree, whereas Euclid's deductions do not allow one to disagree if one has first granted his assumptions.

Now in the last three chapters we have mentioned the name of Hull again and again. He above all others was the person who set up the Law of Effect as an all-embracing principle. But we have managed so far to talk about his views without mentioning the feature of them which some people would think the most important. In many of his papers his psychological theories are set out deliberately according to the model of Euclid, starting by defining terms, then stating some assumed postulates, and finally proceeding by a set of rigorous steps to some conclusion. In one book the argument proceeds primarily in symbolic logic rather than in ordinary English, so as to make sure that no emotional overtones or blurred definitions spoil the reasoning.

Of course, there is one obvious difference between Euclid and Hull. Euclid's assumptions are generally accepted on the basis of everyday experience, and therefore his conclusions can be accepted as facts on the same basis. Hull's assumptions, such as the Law of Effect, are not at all certain *even to him:* and the whole object of his careful argument is to draw conclusions which he can then test by carrying out an experiment. If the result of the experiment is in disagreement with the deduction, it must mean that one of the assumptions of the argument is false. But so long as the experiments agree with the results of the logical argument, one can continue to hold the assumptions as provisionally true. And of course the more predictions turn out to agree with experiment, the more probable the assumptions become. Euclid's theorems have often been thought to show a way of discovering truth by reason without appeal to the evidence of experience: Hull's theorems are quite definitely intended for testing against experience, and, if the facts disagree with some deduction, so much the worse for the assumptions on which the deduction rests.

But in this Hull is merely making something clear which is in fact true also of Euclid. His geometry is accepted because it happens to agree with our everyday experience, rather than contradict it: and if one of his deductions turns out false in some special situation that means that we have to reject Euclid's assumptions for that situation. For instance, if we draw a large triangle on the surface of the Earth we can easily prove that its angles add up to some amount different from two right angles.*

* Think of two men standing at the North Pole: each of them sets off in a direction at right-angles (90°) to the other, and eventually both of them reach the Equator. Each then turns through 90° to face the other and they walk to meet

This means that the surface of the Earth is not a surface for which Euclid's assumptions are true: the reason being that it is of course curved in a third dimension so that lines which are parallel at the Equator can nevertheless meet at the North Pole. Modern physics considers cases in which even three-dimensional space behaves in a non-Euclidean way, as though it were curved in some fourth dimension; and once again we know that Euclid's assumptions must be discarded in such a space, because empirically the facts he deduces turn out to be false.

So there is no real difference between Hull's method and Euclid's. Geometry does not give us truth by pure reason, any more than psychological theories do. Each of them sets up assumptions which have implications, and these implications are then tested against experience. In very many situations Euclidean geometry is in fact applicable: Hull's psychology is less widely successful, but it too has some triumphs to its credit.

## An Example of a Successful Deduction

There is only one way to get the feel of Hull's style, and that is to read his original papers. But it is possible to give an example of the kind of deduction he made, leaving out all the precision of his phrasing.

One of his assumptions was, of course, that the more times a particular response appeared successfully in a situation, the more likely it was to do so again. This tendency-to-respond was supposed to die away as time went on (to account for the facts of forgetting) but the decay with time was assumed to be fairly slow. Even quite a long time after learning had taken place, not much forgetting was supposed to have happened.

On the other hand, another of Hull's assumptions was that each time any response occurred there was a very temporary reluctance to repeat it. This 'inhibitory' tendency was supposed to die away rapidly as time went by: it can be thought of crudely as a kind of

each other. The triangle they have traced out has angles which add up to 270°, that is, three right-angles.

fatigue, which opposes the frequent repetition of an action, but soon disappears with rest. Without this assumption one would have had to predict that learning would be best if it was repeated as often as possible so as to allow no time for forgetting. But in fact this is not so: both human and animal learning of a simple type is best carried out in short and widely spaced bursts. If one wants to learn a poem by heart, with the least number of readings, it is better to read it once only each day rather than to go through it again and again on one occasion until it is mastered. Hull's assumed inhibitory tendency explains this: spacing out the learning allows the fatigue-like inhibition to disappear between each session, and so gives better performance than a series of massed learning sessions with no rests between them.

If now one considers the two assumptions we have mentioned, there is another and unlooked-for consequence of them. When a series of learning sessions ends, there must be quite a marked amount of inhibition present in addition to the positive learning which has been secured. As time passes, the inhibition will die rapidly away, whereas the positive learning will only decay slowly. So the performance of the learner ought to *improve* for a time after he has stopped learning, until all the inhibition has disappeared. After that he will get worse in the ordinary course of forgetting. But in the first place he ought to get better even though he isn't learning.

This certainly sounds contrary to common sense. In addition, the prediction is not easy to test, because obviously if one asks a man to learn something, and then tests his knowledge, the test itself may remind him of some fresh information and so he will do better in another later test. Besides, it is hard to tell just when a man does stop learning; he may put away his book and yet go on repeating the lesson over and over to himself. But an experiment was carried out which tried to overcome these difficulties. The man had to learn nonsense words which were shown one after another through a small opening: when he had practised to a certain point, he was kept fully occupied on another job until the time came to test his knowledge of the nonsense words. One group of people were tested immediately after learning, another quite separate group thirty seconds later, yet another group two minutes after learning, and so on: the people tested at any particular time after learning had not been tested at any previous time. This experiment did show the queer and surprising result that for a minute or two after the end of learning, performance gets better than it was immediately after learning. The test of memory given as soon as learning stops shows a lower score than the one given a little later.

This then is an example of Hull's method: the theory is set up, some prediction is made about facts by logical argument from the theory, and then an experiment is done to test the prediction. If the results support the prediction, the theory is held with greater confidence. One success by itself does not add very much, since a theory as general as Hull's has quite a lot of implications and each of these has to be tested. For instance, the curious effect of improving memory after a rest should only appear if the learning has been carried out in a continuous block without pauses: and in fact this is true. If a man has taken rests during his learning, his performance at the end of the training is as good as it will ever be, and it simply deteriorates in the ordinary fashion of forgetting. Another prediction (which involves other parts of the theory) is that the effect will be bigger in the middle of a list of nonsense words than it is at the beginning or end of the list, and this also is true. The whole network of predictions is supposed to reinforce the group of assumptions forming the theory.

To some extent this technique, which Hull emphasized, is the usual one in other branches of science. Indeed, it might strike people, who are familiar with science in general, as odd that anybody should need to make this method a matter for debate. But there are two reasons which made Hull's attitude notable and controversial. In the first place, psychologists before his day had quite certainly put too little emphasis on the need to test out theories by experiment. They had also, perhaps as a result, been too inclined to leave their theoretical concepts undefined. It took a rather over-emphasized proclamation of the virtues of Hull's method to counteract this laxity and to bring into disrepute any theory which was not intimately connected with experiment.

In the second place, however, it could be argued that some features of Hull's practice were not the same as the method used in other fields of science. As a result he was criticized by some psychologists of strongly experimental and scientific inclinations, as well as by those who reject the behaviourist approach and consequently reject also the whole idea of testing theory by experiments on behaviour. Perhaps the best way of introducing the criticism of Hull's methods is to contrast him with another behaviourist who became celebrated in the Thirties: B. F. Skinner.

## The Rejection of Theory

Hull's theory, as we have seen, supposed that there were competing tendencies to respond and not to respond, fighting it out within a man or an animal. These tendencies could not be directly observed, but were supposed to be revealed by their effects on behaviour. Skinner would reject altogether the use of unobservables: he would say rather that we ought simply to say what we do to the animal, what the animal does in return, and to find out regularities in the relation between these two kinds of observation. Hull supposes that when we stop rewarding an animal for some action the tendency to react ceases to increase: but the tendency *not* to react goes on increasing every time an action occurs and so the animal stops doing things which bring no reward. Skinner would simply state the observation that reward increases the frequency of response, and stopping the reward decreases its frequency; and he would not suppose any invisible inhibitory tendency.

Now the obvious advantage of this attitude of sticking to the facts is that it may cause one to find facts which somebody would miss who was interested only in testing theories. On an everyday level, a man who goes through a beautiful landscape looking for some particular object will notice less of his surroundings than another man will who has no such pre-occupation. Even in experimental situations, one can prove that a man who is briefly shown a picture of several coloured objects will be less likely to notice what the objects are if he has previously been instructed to remember what the colours are. Looking for one thing tends to stop us looking for other things: and so a concern with proving or disproving complicated deductions from theory may stop us noticing interesting facts. Skinner's antagonism to theory should therefore find its justification in the discovery of such interesting facts, and indeed he has contributed a number of intriguing experimental observations. Some of them suggest an answer to the dilemma concerning punishment which we mentioned in Chapter III – punishment tends to produce dangerous conflict, and yet seems indispensable because it produces a kind of learning which is particularly permanent. Skinner has found ways of producing similarly permanent learning using reward.

If we consider a simple action, such as the pressing of a lever by a rat, it is possible to reach a compromise between rewarding the action every time and never rewarding it at all. One can, for instance, give the rat some food every hundredth time it performs the action: or give food only on the first action after the clock strikes each hour of the day. There are many other such possibilities. Skinner has studied a number of them, and shown that quite different behaviour may result from different ways of rewarding an action.

There is, for instance, an important difference between rewarding systematically, after certain times or numbers of actions, and rewarding irregularly. If one gives the reward in a random fashion, sometimes rewarding two or three actions in a row and sometimes leaving a long series of actions unrewarded, the animal will respond at a fairly steady rate which does not speed up or slow down very much after each reward. If however one gives the reward regularly, say for every tenth or hundredth action, the rate of response changes every time the reward is given. Immediately after reward the animal slows down and becomes relatively un-interested in the action that is being rewarded. As time goes on he works faster and faster, until a very high rate of response is reached at about the point where the reward occurs. Then there is another slowing-down, and the whole cycle repeats itself. The same irregular pattern of action appears if reward is only available at certain systematic times.

Besides the distinction between regular and irregular reward, there is an important difference between a system based on time and one based on number of actions. If one rewards the first response after each hour has struck, the animal tends to respond less frequently than he does if one rewards the first response in each minute. The probability of response follows that of reward; so that the less often one rewards, the less active the rat becomes. But if one uses the other possible method and gives the reward after a certain number of actions, the picture becomes quite differ-ent. A rat, which is rewarded every hundredth time it does some-thing, will repeat the action more rapidly than will a rat which is rewarded every tenth action. When the animal's rate of work affects the frequency of reward, then, it seems to be true that the less generous one is with reward the more active the rat becomes.

A third important distinction is between the effect of reward on learning itself, and the effect on subsequent behaviour when the reward is discontinued. If one were to put a completely naïve rat in front of a lever and give it a reward only when it had pressed the lever a hundred times, it would be a very long time before the animal learned to press the lever. One would get far quicker learning by rewarding every pressure on the lever. In fact, even if one wants to end up with the 'one-in-a-hundred' schedule of reward, it is as well to start by rewarding every response until the animal is making the right action fairly frequently: one can then gradually reduce the ratio of reward to actions.

Learning, then, is faster when a high proportion of actions are rewarded. But if one suddenly stops giving reward altogether, the relationship is reversed. The rat which is used to getting a reward every time it presses a lever will soon stop doing so when the reward stops; but the animal which has in the past got a reward only for every hundredth response will go on working for very long periods after reward has stopped. If this seems too surprising at first sight, one should perhaps point out that the rat trained on a low ratio of rewards to actions is more used to producing responses which are not followed by reward. To look at the same point from a slightly different angle, the animal trained on a low ratio treats a hundred responses as equivalent to one of those produced by the high ratio animal. The persistent behaviour which results from a low ratio of reward is just as intelligible as that which results from using punishment to produce learning.

From these various effects of different schedules of reward, it seems that an animal is liable under certain conditions to stop making the right action as soon as it gets a reward; it is liable to make the action more frequently if it has been rewarded for a lower proportion of actions, and it is less likely to go on working unrewarded if it has had a lot of rewards. All these are facts which one would hardly expect on a simple interpretation of the Law of Effect, although they can be fitted into Hull's approach by the exercise of a little ingenuity. (For example, with regular schedules of reward the situation of just-having-been-rewarded is a situation in which responses have not in the past been rewarded). Consequently it seems fair to count the discovery of these facts as a credit to Skinner's policy of sticking to observation and not creating hypothetical principles.

They are certainly important facts. Putting them all together, it seems that we can best get an animal to keep up a high rate of some desired response, if we reward it only infrequently at irregular intervals and make the average interval depend on the actual rate of response. On the human level, it would clearly be wrong to interpret the Law of Effect as meaning that one must strain every nerve to reward a child each time he shows good manners. On the contrary, if any analogy with experiments on learning is permissible, the best educational technique should be something after the following style. First, emphasize the particular behaviour which is wanted by praising and approving every instance of it which appears. But then, once the general connection has been established, make the praise infrequent and irregular. It must not, however, be given at a constant average interval of time, but ought to be responsive to the child's own actions so that more frequent occurrence of the behaviour will obtain more frequent reward. By such means one might hope to encourage desirable actions to the point where the child continues to perform them even when nobody is there to reward him: in fact, irregular reward may do the job (which is very often left to punishment) of producing honest behaviour in the absence of a policeman.

In earlier chapters we considered the disadvantage of punishment so far as conflicts of motives are concerned: conflicts involving punishment are more difficult to resolve. Such an objection should not apply to situations involving irregular reward, and accordingly perhaps we should modify the traditional view that it is better to love good than to fear evil. Perhaps we should say that it is better to love good, and to be accustomed to getting only infrequent reward for doing so.

## Experiments on People

It would be difficult to confirm whether Skinner's rules apply to the training of human beings in moral matters: but it is possible to carry out such researches on the behaviour of people in fields which are less ethically charged, and this has been done. Some of the experiments require no apparatus and can probably be repeated by the reader on his friends. A particularly entertaining study, for example, was that of an American psychologist who counted the number of times people made statements of personal opinion to him. If he reinforced that type of statement, by making some such encouraging remark as 'You're so right' or 'I wish everyone thought like that' whenever a person expressed an opinion, the frequency of remarks of that type increased. Most of the people on whom he performed this experiment were quite unaware of the process; in fact the experimenter himself was studied without his knowledge by somebody else, and showed the same effect. If therefore we are rash enough to make approving noises whenever somebody is laying down the law on a doubtful subject, we have only ourselves to blame if we find we have to listen to the same kind of thing more frequently in future!

A similar but rather easier experiment, is to ask a friend to say in a series whatever words come into his head. If one interrupts and says 'Good' every time he says a plural noun, he will usually say more and more words of that sort. Sometimes he will still be unable to tell what is going on, although some people do realize the principle of the experiment in this case.

More formally, one can build an apparatus which allows a man to see a dial briefly whenever he presses a particular button. If he is told to watch out for a signal on the dial, and if that kind of signal is given according to one of the schedules described by Skinner, the man's button-pressing behaves in the same way as the bar-pressing of rats. When signals are regular, the man does not look for one immediately after he has seen another. If signals are put in at certain times, he looks for them less often the less frequent they are: but if they are put in whenever he has looked a certain number of times, he looks more often the lower the ratio of signals to looks. Skinner's rules of behaviour apply to people just as to animals; they are generalizations rather than simply facts about a particular species. Of course, it could well be argued that the mechanism which makes a rat behave in this way is not the same as that which makes a man do so. We have noted earlier animal actions which might at first sight seem similar to the results of human intelligence, but which are in the animal case merely the result of an instinctive mechanism lacking foresight or reasoning. The difference is concealed by one type of observation and shows up only in special experiments. Equally the identical behaviour of rat and man in Skinner's experiments may be due to different mechanisms. But to the purely outside observer this is unimportant: the invisible is the irrelevant, and from Skinner's point of view it is only the lawful relationship, between behaviour and the schedule of reward, which matters.

## Limitations of Skinner's Approach

The great attraction of sticking purely to observation is that it ought to banish speculation. We know what an animal does: let us not worry about supposed mechanisms which cannot be seen. By ignoring such theoretical guess-work, we shall remain alert to interesting factual relationships such as the curious effects of low ratios of reward. This kind of argument is rightly appealing to one type of scientific mind. Just as some people are impressed by Euclid, others take a delight in raw facts. Long chains of reasoning are apt to err, because of prejudice, misunderstanding, and the blurring of the meaning of words. So some people would rather state simply that when A occurs, B will shortly follow.

Unfortunately, behaviour does not altogether lend itself to rules of that sort. On a simple observational level, an animal placed in the same situation does not always do the same thing. We saw in the last chapter that a rat, who normally responds to the sight of a runway by running eagerly along it, will not do so if he has previously been shocked in the food-box at the far end. B does not follow A if some other event has intervened. On the other hand, animals will produce correct solutions to novel problems, where we cannot establish a rule before the event itself occurs. How can these difficulties be tackled by Skinner's approach?

One method is to confine oneself primarily to those situations which are amenable to simple rules. For example, we can study in more and more detail the behaviour of a rat in a cage containing only one lever which he can press. By considering only the number of times that the lever is pressed, and relating it to the presentation of food, we can then build up laws about behaviour without needing to bother ourselves about the difficulties appearing in experiments on insight.

But this surely is just as restrictive as any theory. If we must make only certain types of observation, our case is no better than that of the man who is so obsessed by his hypothesis that he misses interesting facts. The whole virtue of Skinner's attitude is that it draws attention to the concrete realities of behaviour, and this virtue is lost if one has to leave out of account large regions of animal and human activity. But there is another method of tackling these types of behaviour even though the observed actions show no regular sequence: and that is to regard them merely as rather confused and unwieldy examples of the working of principles which can be established in the more restricted experiments. This after all is sometimes the method of physical scientists, who experiment in artificially constrained situations but happily use the results to explain everyday phenomena such as rainbows, soap-bubbles, or thunder-storms. Following this example, Skinner himself, and some of his colleagues, would use the principles of behaviour found in their experiments to explain more everyday actions such as speech, which do not form perfectly regular and invariant sequences. One can do this by picking out some of the features of the everyday situation and saying that they are equivalent to particular features of the laboratory one. For instance, when a rat is rewarded for action only when a red light is present and not rewarded in the presence of a green one, the action soon appears only to the red light. Skinner would say that when a man is phrasing a logical argument, the earlier words in the argument correspond to the red light for a rat: in their presence only certain utterances (the logically correct ones) have been rewarded and therefore the man does not follow one phrase by another which is inconsistent with the first. When we say 'All men are mortal and Socrates is a man' we are on this view producing a situation in which the rewarded response has in the past been of the type 'Socrates is mortal' and that is why we draw the correct conclusion. (It is of course not necessary to suppose that we have met the particular argument before, only the general form of words.)

In more difficult cases, it is possible to connect complex and apparently inexplicable behaviour with simple laboratory situations by supposing that controlling stimuli or rewards exist but happen not to be noticeable. For instance, Skinner explains certain slips in everyday speech very much as Freud does, by saying that the speaker has an underlying preoccupation and that this would normally produce the word which suddenly intrudes in a conversation on some quite different subject. If I say 'So long, I must fry', when I mean to say 'fly', the reason may be that I am hungry.

The snag with this method is that it loses all the merit of Skinner's empiricism. Speculation is just as bad when it concerns stimuli and rewards as it is when it concerns imageless thought or mixed feelings: one does not make an account of behaviour objective merely by using words borrowed from experimental situations. Other people might analyse verbal behaviour in other ways: any particular slip of the tongue could be due to an underlying preoccupation or to the effect of immediately preceding words acting like the red light to a rat or any combination of the two factors. How are we to distinguish between alternative interpretations? Unless we get evidence from the actual situation we are trying to interpret, one guess is as good as another: and when we try to examine that actual situation, we find that we are using something very like Hull's method of putting up a theory and then looking to see if consequences predicted from the theory are true.

Skinner's method therefore runs us into a dilemma. If we want to stick to the idea of studying the rules of observed behaviour, we have to leave out a lot of actions which, like human speech or animal problem-solving, do not form simple repeating sequences. If on the other hand, we want to include these kinds of behaviour by means of the laws found in simpler situations, we have to say just which part of the complicated behaviour corresponds to which part of the simple case. As this can be done in various ways, we shall simply be guessing if we do no experiments on the complicated case itself. And when applied to complex behaviour, rules drawn from simple situations are theories just as much as the excitatory and inhibitory tendencies of Hull are.

These difficulties lead us back to a more fundamental point in Skinner's attitude. He is concerned with complete regularity, with

the *control* of behaviour by particular stimuli or particular rewards. The laws he seeks are not statistical; when we mentioned
earlier the differences between reward given on a time basis and
reward given after a certain number of responses, these were intended to be true of any rat one cares to study. Many of Skinner's
own experiments are in fact carried out only on one or two
animals rather than examining a large number and studying the
average performance of the group. Now in this he and his followers are in marked contrast to the rest of modern experimental
psychology. So far in this book we have not mentioned the actual
techniques used by experimenters in finding the results quoted.
But the usual method is in fact to make a number of observations,
to work out mathematically the odds against the results being due
to chance, and to accept the findings as fact only if the odds against
chance are very heavy. For example, suppose we are teaching a
rat a maze which offers it the choice of two pathways, a left and a
right. We might put saccharin in one path, and see if the rat
tended to choose that path. But if it does, we cannot immediately
say that 'rats like saccharin' because there were only two choices
and therefore the odds were even as between the two paths. If
however, we studied ten rats and all of them chose the saccharin
path, the odds are five hundred to one against such a conclusive
result being obtained by sheer chance: and therefore we probably
would say 'rats like saccharin'.

This kind of method, in more sophisticated forms, is used very
widely. Usually the results are less one-sided than in the example.
An experimenter will announce a finding although perhaps
twenty per cent of his animals did not behave in the same way as
the rest. The reason for thinking that this is fair is that all sorts of
chance factors must affect these experiments – the animals may
have learned other things previously without one's knowledge, or
some chance smell or sound may reach the experimental room
from one side or the other and bias certain animals. So the behaviour of the majority is very often taken as the 'true' behaviour
of all, chance factors explaining the minority results.

Skinner's results on the other hand are intended to display relationships which are not disturbed by chance factors. By rigid control and by choosing the right things to measure, he would claim one can get beyond the uncertainty of statistics and reach the fundamental laws of behaviour. In this as in so much else, Skinner's attitude makes a great appeal to some kinds of scientist. Surely it is clumsy to let errors creep into experiments and then get rid of them by statistics? How much better to do research properly on one animal rather than badly on twenty! And one must admit that Skinner does possess such insight into behaviour that many of the results he describes are really true of any animal. But there are three criticisms which can be made of his hostility to statistics.

In the first place, one can never be sure if one has controlled every relevant factor in an experiment on behaviour, until it has been repeated and shown the same result. Indeed the same is to some extent true in the physical sciences. But when one is dealing with intact animals, the possibility of intruding errors is so serious that the precaution of 'having another look' needs to be taken every time. Even if one is right in thinking that one has analysed a fundamental law of behaviour, rather than a chance feature of a particular animal, there is no way to check this without studying a number of animals. It is therefore very dangerous to concentrate on a few specimens.

Secondly, there are some kinds of behaviour which disappear under controlled conditions: if we exclude all stray sounds and smells, the animal may act in a different way from that which he would use in more normal conditions. In an earlier chapter we mentioned the possibility that learning the difference between two alleyways is a more complex process when there are more features, which might possibly, from the animal's point of view, be the ones to be learned. It is therefore worth while to study behaviour even under conditions so loose that a minority of the results turn out the wrong way.

Lastly, and most seriously, it is possible and indeed likely, that the variability of behaviour is its crucial feature. There would be no evolution of species without the chance factors which cause each individual animal to differ slightly from its neighbour: equally there might well be no learning without the chance factors which make each response different from its neighbour. Although it is valuable to pick out some strictly determined laws of behaviour, it is also worth while to study the laws of its variation: and these must be statistical.

For these reasons, then, Skinner's attractive scheme of discarding theory altogether, and sticking to deterministic laws of behaviour, is not convincing to everybody. Either it leaves out most of behaviour, or it lands us in speculation: and it tends to ignore the value of the statistical approach. Nevertheless it is a valuable antidote to overdeveloped theories, and is worth keeping in mind when we go on to consider other approaches.

## Limitations of Hull's Approach

At least the method introduced by Hull does not suffer from the same difficulties as that of Skinner. Any field of behaviour, no matter how complex, can be studied by means of the setting up of a theory and the testing of predictions drawn from it. Most psychologists in the Forties professed great respect for Hull's approach, even if they disagreed with the kind of theory he used for his predictions. Just like Euclid, he carried with him an aura of precision which gave his writings great status. In very recent times however, the pendulum has rather swung towards Skinner's approach, and relatively little research is being done in the Hullian manner. This may seem surprising since, as we have just seen, there are some fields which are difficult to study without a theory and Hull's use of theory seems so much in the tradition of other fields of science. It is still too soon to be clear about the reasons for the present unfashionableness of Hull, but the rest of this chapter will offer a few suggestions.

In the first place, a number of criticisms of Hull's own theory (as opposed to his method) have appeared. At least four main kinds of criticism can be distinguished. (1) In the last chapter we mentioned Deutsch's point that 'fractional anticipatory goal responses' could not obey the general Law of Effect, since otherwise a thirsty rat would go to places where it had been fed. (2) The idea of the inhibitory tendency, which, like fatigue, arises from every action and dies away with rest, also ran into difficulties. It was supposed to explain why unrewarded actions died out: but certain experiments showed that lack of reward could have an effect even though the action never occurred at all. For instance, showing a rat that the food-box at the end of a maze is empty will impair his speed through the maze just as if one had let him run through the maze and find the empty box for himself. (3) The Law of Effect itself had to be modified until, as we have seen, Spence made it disappear almost altogether. (4) At the same time critics were pointing out that some of Hull's very complex mathematical predictions were tested only by experiments giving fairly crude results, so that the facts forming the basis and justification for the theory were more slender than the complicated edifice created upon them. It is rather as though one were trying to explain the workings of a clock by making a complete drawing of the mechanism by guess-work without looking inside; and then supporting this guess by pointing out that the supposed mechanism would tick and that the clock does in fact tick. The test needs to be stiffer.

Because of these criticisms, many psychologists have tended either to side with Skinner or else to hold that, while Hull's method was correct, a different set of hypotheses are needed. One might argue however, that some third attitude is possible. It might, for instance, be that Hull's method is not completely correct despite its resemblance to that of other sciences: it needs some alteration if it is not to lead to speculation. The flaw, which in the writer's opinion endangers any theory built in the Hullian way, is the neglect of alternative theories. In the example of the clock, the trouble is that many different mechanisms would predict a tick, and so the presence of the tick does not really justify us in picking on one of those mechanisms. Equally, wherever a theory is set up and tested by experimental predictions, the tests must be such that they are not explained by alternative theories. We have to find experiments in which everybody else's theory predicts one thing to happen, but our theory predicts another.

Of course, this is a tall order. At the beginning of the last chapter the argument between Tolman and Miller was described, in which an experiment (thought by Tolman to be crucial) was shown by Miller to have the same predicted result whichever theory one held. This is a typical case. By sufficient ingenuity one can reconcile many experimental results with almost any of the theories current in psychology. Each theory includes numerous concepts and provides a variety of mechanisms, one of which is sure to fit the particular situation. This is not unreasonable, if we think that the role of a theory is to explain all the features of behaviour; for the true explanation is bound to be a complicated one when we ultimately discover it. If therefore one sets out to guess at the explanation, and check the guess by experiment, it has to be a complicated guess. But, to give a personal opinion again, this in itself condemns the 'guess-and-check' method (or 'hypothetico-deductive' as it tends to be known). The checks become impossible with complicated guesses.

What then should the answer be? As far as possible one ought to keep one's theorizing at a level of complication at which the checks still distinguish one theory from another. For instance, to return to the analogy of the clock, it would be quite legitimate to argue on the following lines. 'The mechanism is probably intermittent, with some pendulum or balance-wheel. The alternative is a very carefully timed continuous motion as with an electric motor. In the former case a tick may be detected and in the latter it is less likely. Let us now listen to the clock.' Hearing a tick would then increase the probability of an intermittent mechanism rather than an electric one. This may not seem as impressive an achievement as the drawing of a complete speculative mechanism. But if one argues in this way one is not likely to make the mistake of thinking that a tick supports a pendulum theory as opposed to a balance-wheel. By keeping the theory general rather than specific, it remains possible to keep in touch with experiment. When a crucial experiment cannot be designed, the theories have become unreal and rarefied.

This therefore is the modification which ought perhaps to be applied to the hypothetico-deductive method: enough guesses should be made, and each should be broad enough, that they cover all the possibilities, and then the checks decide between them. But one must admit that something in scientific method escapes from such a rule: some people are better at analysing the problem, at guessing, than others are, and in the end theorists of scientific method are simply looking at the work of these masters and trying to put their methods into words. A good deal is lost between the original and its description, and therefore it is not a good idea to read a philosophical book about scientific method and then to start research with no other background. There is as yet no substitute for working with other more experienced researchers and acquiring the feel of scientific method in an intuitive way. The foregoing analysis of the flaw in Hull's method may therefore be quite mistaken: but there is nevertheless a widespread feeling that a flaw does exist, and that theory had somehow got out of hand in the hypothetico-deductive technique.

## Concerning Events within the Skull

Both Hull and Skinner agree on one thing: they are not dealing with events in the brain but only with behaviour. One of them confines himself simply to observation, and the other sets up general abstract principles and deduces consequences from them. But neither of them says 'the animal acts in this way because such-and-such groups of cells in the nervous system are stimulated'. There are two reasons for this absence of the brain from their accounts of behaviour. The first is that they are both proponents of the view that behaviour by itself is a sufficient field to form a separate science. While physiology no doubt has connections with that field, they can be left until the main structure of a science of behaviour has been built. The second reason for avoiding physiological explanations is that in fact and to some extent in principle, they are speculative. Nobody really knows what happens in the brain when even simple actions occur. So although it may seem very scientific to talk about nerves and areas in the brain, this is really deceptive. It is almost as bad to say that emotion is due to impulses travelling up from the lower centres of the nervous system to the surface of the brain, as it is to say that emotion involves no conscious experience other than sensations of bodily change. We dealt in the first chapter with the objections to the second of these statements. But the first is almost more dangerous, because people who use words derived from experiments tend to forget that there is no experimental backing for this particular combination of those words.

In discussing the validity of physiological explanations, behaviourists have leaned heavily upon modern advances in physics which we mentioned earlier. If concepts are defined only by the operations of observing them, so that one cannot have a velocity without a specified method of measuring it, then a concept like 'amount of learning' or 'degree of fatigue' can only be made meaningful in terms of behaviour. One can say that this animal has learned more than that one has, because under specified conditions their actions differ: and this is the only meaning that can be attached to 'amount of learning'. It is an 'intervening variable' useful for simplifying conversation but having no real existence. If one were to treat it as something real, to look for example at the number of nervous connections in the two animals and expect to find a parallel to amount of learning, one would be said to regard it as a 'hypothetical construct' rather than an intervening variable. Most behaviourists seem to feel that giving such an aura of real existence to their concepts is unwarrantable, just as many modern physical concepts must not be regarded as having a real existence.

But this is too limiting. In physics certain concepts are ruled out as meaningless because the very nature of observation makes it impossible even to give them an operational definition. For instance a velocity without a frame of reference is such a concept: as soon as one started to measure, one would have to adopt a frame. But this is not true of the brain. At the moment we cannot observe the impulses travelling from lower to higher centres when a man says he feels an emotion: but there is no reason in principle why advancing knowledge should not produce a technique for us to do so. If therefore we state a theory in terms of nerve cells and connections, it is not really meaningless but merely rather difficult to confirm. It is important to remember that we do not guarantee scientific respectability by using physiological words; but equally there is nothing against making our guesses in those words when we see the opportunity, and getting physiological checks as well as psychological ones.

To summarize this theoretical chapter, each of the extreme points of view on scientific method is probably unjustified although each of them makes an important point. If we stick purely to looking at behaviour, we have to exclude complex actions such as problem-solving where the crucial events seem to occur inside the nervous system. If we guess what those events are, we are likely to get too speculative unless we also try to think out what the other alternatives are and to pick experiments for deciding between them. Lastly, we have to beware of thinking that statements about nervous connections are necessarily more scientific than the Law of Effect, but equally we ought to remember that behaviour depends on the brain: and that therefore it may sometimes be useful to put our theories in a form which can be tied down to physiology. With this in mind, let us now turn to knowledge about the effects of brain damage on behaviour.

# 6

# A Scalpel in the Works

The most outstanding fact about the brain, and the one which is least often considered by amateur theorists, is its extraordinary resistance to damage. It is perfectly possible for a man to have considerable injury from a tumour or a blow, or even to have a bullet pass completely through his brain, and still to behave sufficiently normally to pass casual inspection. Most machines built by human beings are quite different in this respect: the removal of any one part is immediately noticed and may disable the machine completely. It is not easy therefore to think of analogies for the functioning of the brain.

Although this fact can be noticed in clinical experience (since men do suffer accidental head injuries) it did not really penetrate behaviourist opinion until Lashley carried out some experiments on the topic around 1930. Before then many people seem to have thought of the brain as a kind of telephone switchboard, in which an incoming message from one of the senses was connected across to a pathway going out to the muscles, so that each stimulus produced an appropriate response. The making of the connections was the process of conditioning. But in a telephone switchboard the connection is localized, and damage to the right part of the board will cut off any particular subscriber from the person who is calling him. It ought therefore to be possible, if this view were true, to find a crucial part of the brain which could be cut out and cause forgetting of the particular habit concerned. This Lashley attempted to do.

Before describing his experiments, we ought to point out that the broad structure of the brain is not too wildly unreasonable on a switchboard model. The nerves from the various senses can be traced upwards to various parts of the cortex, which is the sheet of cells forming a kind of dome over the top of the nervous system. Nerves from the eye go to an area of the cortex which is inside the back of the head, nerves from the ear to an area inside the side of the head, and so on. Outgoing nerves to the muscles can also be traced back, to a strip lying across the top of the head. So one could think of these areas as corresponding on a switchboard to the rows of sockets for incoming and outgoing calls, and the nerve cells of the cortex in between the areas might correspond to the wires criss-crossing the front of the board. There are therefore two kinds of damage that might be particularly interesting: injury to the 'projection areas' where the nerves arrive, and injury to the parts of the cortex between the sensory and motor areas. Both kinds of injury might affect a habit which had already been learned, but relearning might well be possible if the projection area was intact: if one cuts a cord or damages a socket on a switchboard the result is in either case to break the connection, but a new cord can substitute for the old one. In addition to these various possibilities, it is as well to try various degrees of complexity in the habits being studied. Accordingly Lashley taught his rats simple and complex discriminations and mazes of varying difficulty.

## The Puzzling Results of Lashley

If we consider first the results on simple discrimination, in which the rats had to learn to go to a lighted compartment as opposed to a dark one, we find that the results are almost (but not exactly) the opposite of those to be expected on the switchboard analogy. A rat can learn this discrimination without its visual projection area, but if it loses the area after it has learned the habit, it will forget which compartment to approach and will have to be retrained. Injury anywhere else in the brain did not affect the habit. So in terms of the switchboard analogy, instead of finding that retention of the habit can be lost when either the cords or the sockets are destroyed, we find that only the sockets are important for old connections: and a *new* connection can be made even without the socket. Incidentally, no particular part of the visual area contained the memory of the discrimination: the loss of memory grew progressively worse as more and more of the area was cut out.

If the discrimination is made a little more complicated by lighting both compartments and rewarding the animal only for going to the brighter one, learning as well as retention of the habit suffered when the visual area was removed. This suggests that the damage to the brain was affecting the extent to which the visual information was getting into the system: a blind rat naturally cannot learn visual patterns nor show that it remembers the ones it learned before it lost its sight. Such an explanation is not necessarily inconsistent with the results on the simple discrimination. For instance, we now know that any stimulus applied to the sense-organs produces general repercussions in a number of parts of the cortex through secondary and indirect pathways, separate from the main nerves running to the projection areas. The animal with no visual area might possibly therefore learn to discriminate the presence or absence of this general non-specific activity according to the presence or absence of light. Such a mechanism would not allow the animal to react to fine differences, but would allow it to compensate for the loss of ordinary visual information. If this were the mechanism, the rat would not be seeing by a different path, but rather using a quite different type of information. The case would be analogous to that of blind human beings, who often learn to make use of reflected sound in order to localize objects which normal people can only detect by vision. A particularly interesting feature of this re-learning is that the blind man himself often does not know how he is aware that a chair or table is in his way. One has to prove that he is using hearing by such means as putting ear-plugs on him or placing him in a sound-absorbing room to alter the character of the echoes.

The main point of the discrimination experiments is, however, that no place outside the visual area was found where the learned response could be cut out. The same point is made even more forcibly by the results of the maze experiments. In this case, the animals were taught mazes of various degrees of difficulty and then had parts of their cortex removed. There was no place which could be said to carry 'the memory of the maze': the extent to which the rat forgot the maze depended on the sheer weight of cortex which was removed but not on the place from which it was removed. The same relationship applied to the learning of fresh mazes: and the effect of losing a given proportion of the brain was greater if the maze was more difficult. Incidentally, even rats with four-fifths of their cortex missing showed some ability to learn, which is a tribute to the resilience of the brain. One will get very little performance from a car or a radio set with four out of five of its components removed!

These results gave a staggering blow to any simple hope of plotting out sections of the brain like a human filing system. It seemed rather that the whole mass of nerve cells formed an undifferentiated whole, any and every part of which could be concerned in a particular habit. Other results on the motor rather than the sensory projection areas tended to give the same impression. It could be shown for instance, that electrical stimulation of part of the motor area (from which the fibres go to the muscles) would produce a certain movement. But next day stimulation of the same part would give a different movement. If one mapped out the motor area on the brain of one animal, it would prove quite different in another specimen: and if part of the area was destroyed the animal might indeed be partly paralysed for a while, but it could often relearn the use of the paralysed limbs. All this evidence argued against the importance of any particular nerve cell or even any region in the organization of the cortex.

## Theories of the Brain as a Whole

In an earlier chapter we mentioned the theory, stemming from

Köhler and his associates, that the outside world was mirrored in a pattern of activity within the nervous system; and that the successful solution of a problem was due to the restructuring of this pattern under the forces inherent in the relationship between the parts. This theory was greatly encouraged by the findings of Lashley, although as we shall see some of his later work had quite the opposite effect. Yet in the Thirties the first impact of the finding, that no particular nerve cell seemed important, was to encourage the theoretical approach which regarded only patterns as crucial. The incoming messages from the senses were thought of as setting up fields of electrical potential on the cortex, and these fields produced changes of potential in the motor area which gave rise to the appropriate response. The field did not depend on the existence of any cell or region: on the other hand it could be prevented from coming into existence, by interference with the sensory projection area. And it could be disturbed to a greater and greater extent by progressive removal of the mass of cells on which it was based: just as a whirlpool in a stream does not depend on any individual drop of water, but does depend on the flow of all the drops and also on a sufficient width in the channel of the stream.

Another source of support for this view came from experiments on human perception. The striking feature of perception, emphasized more and more by experiments during the period between the Wars, is that we do not experience any sensations which are mere isolated effects of particular stimuli. Rather we relate each part of our field of view to all the other parts and respond to the whole pattern. For example, we can identify the colour of an object with surprising accuracy under illumination of various colours provided that we can see other objects around it in the same illumination. If we look at the object completely on its own, without seeing the surroundings or the light, we cannot judge its colour. But the effect of the surroundings is not a matter of conscious inference, since we can remove and replace them repeatedly and see the test object change colour despite our knowledge that it is still the same. In the same way we see objects as a particular size and shape because of the framework of other objects around them and not because the image formed inside our eyes actually has that size and shape. The eye itself acts like a camera: but any amateur photographer knows that a man-made camera will show distant objects as far smaller than they seem to human perception. Many an enchanting view to the eye is to the camera merely a vast expanse of grass with a tiny strip of scenery at the far end. It requires considerable training to see a scene as the camera would see it, with the size of each object determined by the size of the area it stimulates in the eye, and not influenced by the rest of the field of view.

Other examples of the way in which perception handles the whole field of view, are the 'blind spot' and the continuity of colour to the edge of the eye. The blind spot is the place where the nerve emerges from the back of the eye. As there can be no sense organs at that point, there is a spot in each eye which is blind. If you close your left eye and look with the other eye rather to the left of some small distant object, you will find that the object disappears. From our present point of view the interesting thing is that the object must be small; as soon as it is large enough for part of it to stick out of the blind spot, it can all be seen. We do not go about with a moving hole in our field of view. It is filled in as far as our experience is concerned on the basis of information drawn from other parts of the eye.

The question of colour at the edge of the eye is illustrated by looking up at a blue summer sky. It looks blue right to the edge of the eye; but we know that there are no sense organs sensitive to colour at the edge, as one can easily prove by getting a friend to bring an unfamiliar object in slowly from one side while one looks straight ahead. It is difficult to tell the colour of the object until it is getting quite near to the point at which one is looking, the exact distance depending on the size and colour of the particular object. When we see colour evenly all over the sky, it is because our perception of events in the corner of our eyes is being influenced by those in central vision.

These are only a few examples of the experiments on perception which had accumulated by the Thirties. They had shaken the confidence of psychologists in the old philosophical tradition that our experience is basically of isolated sensations and that more complex percepts are built up by learning. The alternative view was that each fibre of the sensory nerves merely contributed a part of a total pattern, which pattern left no part isolated and unaffected. The experience which people describe when they introspect was based on the pattern and not on the original parts. The same concept of pattern could explain both the curious results of brain injury and the integrated character of perception.

## The Arguments against Fields of Potential in the Brain

There were, even in the Thirties, reasons for feeling unhappy about the theory just described. It had just become clear that the nerves running between the senses and the brain on the one hand, and the brain and the muscles on the other, act in rather a peculiar way. They are not like telephone wires, for instance. They are much more like trains of gunpowder. The only way a message can travel along one is in a sudden wave of activity sweeping from one end to the other: and, just as with gunpowder, the size of the wave at one end has no relation to the size at the other. It may be bigger or smaller depending on the local situation: on how much gunpowder there is in this part of the train. The nerve either fires off a pulse in this way or it does not. There is no intermediate way of conducting a message, and the only way in which a particular fibre can react differently to two different stimuli is by altering the number of pulses which travel along it in a given time. In sensory nerves, for instance, a brighter light or a heavier pressure will give a more rapid series of pulses than fainter stimuli would. But each pulse is the same whatever the nature of the stimulus.

Now if the nerve cells in the cortex act in this same way, on the All-Or-None Law as it is called, they would not seem to provide a very good basis for the theory of fields of potential in the brain. The size of the pulse at each point would not have anything to do with the stimulus, nor could one think of the cells as being in a stationary state like the plates of an electrical condenser. There is no proof that the cells of the cortex do work in the same way as the more easily accessible cells which reach out to the periphery of the body: but it is reasonable to suppose that they do, and if so it is difficult to see how they could produce any patterns of potential. There is also a rather suspicious vagueness about the way in which the occurrence of a pattern selects the appropriate response: and in general the theory was not one which commended itself to physiologists working on the nervous system from their own point of view. Nevertheless the evidence of Lashley's experiments and of the numerous results on perception seemed so strong that no direct attack on the theory was made for some time.

Towards the end of the Forties, however, a major assault developed. On the one hand, Lashley and his associates produced some new experiments aimed directly at the theory of fields of potential: and on the other hand D. O. Hebb put forward an alternative explanation which supposed the cells in the cortex to work in the same way as those elsewhere in the nervous system. The experimental attack consisted simply of fastening strips of electrical conducting material across the visual projection area of a rat, and then testing his ability to distinguish shapes visually. Any field of potential ought to be badly disturbed by this treatment, as if one had poked a pin through a soap-bubble. But the rat remained obstinately able to discriminate shapes. It was equally useless to cut slits in the cortex and insert strips of insulating material, which ought also to distort any potential field. So the simple form of the field theory cannot be upheld, and Lashley had cancelled out the boost which his earlier experiments gave to that theory.

Hebb's contribution was mainly theoretical: he put forward an alternative to the field theory, explaining the same facts without assuming any special properties for cells in the cortex. He treated the cells simply as units, each of which would give a burst of activity when suitably stimulated, just as the cells in the sensory nerves do. In addition, he added the assumption that whenever two cells in contact with each other fire off in rapid succession, an increasing degree of contact develops between them so that the firing of one cell will in future tend to set off the next. There is some, not completely conclusive, physiological evidence that this may be so.

Hebb then considered, on the basis of these assumptions, what would happen if the brain was to consist at birth simply of a random mass of cells with connections coming into and out of it at certain points. There would clearly be a tendency, if any pattern of stimuli was repeatedly presented to the senses, for the cells stimulated by one part of the pattern to fire off at the same time as those stimulated by other parts. Accordingly they would rapidly become connected so that the arousal of any part of the pattern would tend to arouse the rest. The response of the brain to stimulation of any particular sense-organ would therefore depend on the presence or absence of stimulation elsewhere. One can see how this would affect, for example, the blueness of the sky. From our earliest days it has been true that whenever we look at a surface with no apparent gradient of colour, sharp contour, or other in-homogeneity on it, our central vision has detected the same colour whichever part of the surface we looked at. Accordingly, when the edge and the centre of the eye have in the past been stimulated by such a surface, the central part of the eye has repeatedly and often moved to study the region of the surface which originally stimulated the edge: and the colour found there has been the same as in the original central position. Therefore the cells in the brain corresponding to that colour will have fired off shortly after the original stimulation. In the adult, therefore, colour will be perceived in connection with the whole of a homogeneous surface even though it is only the central part of the eye which can detect what colour it is.

Another consequence of Hebb's assumptions is that an equivalence would develop, through learning, between different sense-organs (say, between different parts of the eye) so that no one of them will be essential. Because of the nature of the world, any object seen by one part of our eye is likely to be seen soon afterwards by another part. As we move about the world nothing is presented suddenly as a stationary stimulus to one group of sense-organs: rather it slides across the field of view so that when we glance over a square table-top, it starts by producing activity in one group of nerve fibres and ends by producing it in quite another group: having fired off a number of others on the way. The cells stimulated by the square pattern on one part of the eye will therefore fire very shortly before those stimulated by the same pattern from another part, and will soon tend to become interconnected until a square stimulus in any part of the eye will fire off the same cells as a square stimulus in other parts. When this stage of learning has been reached, it is truly the pattern rather than any particular element which is important. If the brain were organized in this way, one could destroy quite large parts of the visual projection area without destroying learning of the difference between two patterns – although removing it all would cause loss of learning. This, of course, is very consistent with Lashley's results on discrimination.

Hebb has therefore provided a possible account of the perception of patterns. What about Lashley's other results on maze learning? These are, in a way, even more puzzling than those on discrimination, since there is not even a particular region of the brain which is associated with the memory. Hebb's account would be somewhat as follows. The groups of cells which correspond to particular visual patterns tend, simply through chance factors, to be near the visual projection areas. If I make friends on a chance basis with people in my home town, the most likely friends will be those who live near to me. But the cells corresponding to a given visual pattern will also be linked with others arising from touch and hearing: when we see a smooth square object, it feels different from a rough round one. Large-scale linking of cells will therefore take place, which will be less tied to certain regions because they involve various projection areas originally, and are in any case more remote from the incoming sensory information. The friends of my friends will be quite widely scattered away from my house.

In addition the connections involved between a visual and a tactual pattern will probably go by a number of different routes. It is worth mentioning here that just after a nerve cell has fired it becomes temporarily more difficult to fire. So if one sees and feels a table once, a connection between two groups of cells may be made by one path: and yet when one sees and feels the table again the cells in the connecting path may happen to be out of action and some new path has to be opened. This new path is likely to be, for the reasons given in the last paragraph, through part of the brain quite different from that used for the first path. So when we are thoroughly familiar with a table, a glance at it may arouse groups of cells originally stimulated by all kinds of sense-organs – but the connections will be multiple and involve a lot of different bits of the brain.

If this were so, cutting out any one part of the brain would hardly be expected to cause an animal to forget something as complex as a maze. In learning the correct path it has used sight, touch, smell, and other senses as well: and the activity set up by each sense has been interconnected so that any sense will substitute for any other and the removal of one set of connections is likely to leave some parallel set quite unaffected. Although Hebb's theory is based on learning taking place through the association of small, separate and localized elements, there is no doubt that a brain acting in accordance with his principles would perform as a whole with only a very general degree of localization of function into different parts. He has therefore succeeded in putting up a theory alternative to that of fields of potential.

## Experiments Arising from Hebb's Theory

The effect of this theory is to make us look at learning from a new angle. Most of us naturally tend to think of the knowledge gained by experience as being knowledge of the association of objects: knives are sharp, this road leads to London, the square on the hypotenuse is equal to the sum of the squares on the other sides of the triangle. In this sense there has long been no doubt that perception contains more than experience can give us. To go back to earlier examples, we can tell the colour of an object in various illuminations even when that object is one we have never seen before. Pilots can judge size and distance reasonably correctly even when landing on an aerodrome which is quite strange to them. The qualities of a thing are not perceived because they have previously been associated with it; and therefore there was a tendency before Hebb's theory appeared, to argue that perception must be due to inborn mechanisms. On Hebb's view, however, the mechanisms themselves may be acquired by slow and tedious learning, and then applied rapidly to quite new situations. It may be necessary to learn the equivalence of objects seen with different parts of the eye, but, once it has been learned, one can see an object on the left and yet recognize it immediately the first time it appears on the right. It may be necessary to learn how to compensate for the colour of illumination, and yet, once it has been learned, one can apply that compensation to judging the hue of a completely strange object.

A number of lines of research immediately suggest themselves. Hebb himself pointed out the importance of examining people who had been born blind and then gained sight as the result of a later operation. How well can they see? Do they need to build up connections before they can recognize patterns? Hebb himself felt that the evidence was reasonably favourable to his own view, because there is no doubt that people of this type have much greater difficulty than the man in the street would imagine. They often cannot recognize by sight objects which they know quite well by touch, and if fairly old when the operation occurs, may show rather little interest in sight as compared with other more familiar senses. Unfortunately it is a little difficult to draw firm conclusions from these cases; partly because few of them have been properly studied. It would of course be most important to experiment in the first few hours of sight, but usually the psychologist does not reach the patient so soon. There are also great difficulties of language, which emphasize the points about introspection made in the first chapter. A man who cannot name an object may, for all we can tell, be able to see it quite normally but simply fail to associate it with the name he has in the past given to something he could feel. On the other hand, his failure to name it might mean that his visual world is simply a complete confusion. It is difficult to distinguish these possibilities, but there is a distinct suspicion that the first is the case. If so, Hebb's view would be less well supported than in the second case.

On the other hand, it may well be dangerous to argue from adults about the learning of babies. Hebb would expect people born blind to have built up a complex network of cells corresponding to combinations of other sensory stimuli, and this network could organize and interconnect the new visual information much faster than a baby's brain could perform the same task. It is an essential part of Hebb's attitude that later learning is built upon the mechanisms established by early learning: unless we have the general concept of knives we cannot learn that they are sharp nor can we get that general concept without having learned to perceive individual objects, nor can we perceive objects without having learned the equivalence of visual patterns in different parts of the eye, and so on. A failure of learning at any point makes later stages impossible, and conversely the considerable learning of a blind man using his other senses may assist him in learning to see. It is also relevant that one can only operate on people whose eyes have not degenerated, and this usually means that they have received some blurred visual stimulation all their lives through the defective parts later put right by operation. Even this vague sensation of light and darkness may be enough to give some visual learning and so make these cases bad sources of evidence. They need further study however.

From what has just been said, it is obvious that the effects of early experience on later learning are also of great interest. For instance, one could try bringing up animals in the dark and then teaching them to go to one visual pattern and avoid another. Unfortunately if this is done the eyes of the animals degenerate so that one cannot expect them to do as well at visual tasks as comparison animals, brought up under normal conditions, will do. But it is possible to restrict the environment during infancy, to make the cages very plain and simple without a lot of interesting visual patterns to be studied. If this is done the adults are less able to learn that one test pattern is associated with reward and another is not. On the other hand, if rats are brought up in a cage with two cards hanging on the wall, each card having a different shape on it, they are able when adult to learn to choose one of the cards more rapidly than rats will who have not had this early experience. This is particularly interesting because it seems to be a case of learning which is not rewarded in the ordinary sense, although it would be possible to argue that different responses to each of the cards were acquired in infancy and rewarded by the ordinary course of feeding.

A slightly similar experiment can be carried out on people, although in that case we are undoubtedly dealing with brains which have already learned a very great deal. In this experiment one might give two groups of people a series of pictures each of which have all sorts of features. There might for instance, be pictures in different colours, with different kinds of objects in them, with different numbers of objects, and so on. The person being studied has to pick out which pictures are 'right' and which are 'wrong'. The experimenter may, for instance, have decided in advance that all red pictures are 'right' and black ones 'wrong', and he tells his victim whether each choice is correct or not. Then he waits to see how many choices have to be made before the red cards are always chosen. The difference between the two groups of people is that both of them have previously taken part in a similar experiment, but that for one group the right answer in that case was, say, that all pictures of living things were 'right' and of inanimate ones 'wrong'. The second group on the other hand, had previously had black pictures 'right' and red ones 'wrong', that is, exactly the opposite to the new problem. But the second group will usually learn quicker than the first, as if it was a help to be accustomed to picking out the red cards from the black ones even though they were previously picked out for rejection. There are various possible explanations for this effect, but some of them have been ruled out by other experiments and the most likely explanation is one in accordance with Hebb's theory: namely, that distinctive internal responses have been built up to redness and blackness, and these assist further learning.

On a less abstract level, the importance of very early experience to human beings is certainly great. There is a tendency for children who lived all their lives in institutions to show less ability to learn than others do who are brought up in the more stimulating atmosphere of a family. This fact, which is fairly well-established, is more often discussed as evidence of the importance of forming a strong emotional link to some individual while one is a baby, but there may be a more purely intellectual element as well. Too many orphanages in our society are lacking both in opportunities for the child to develop emotional links, and also in chances for him to meet a variety of experiences and so build up a suitable basis for further learning. Slightly different action will need to be taken to meet the two kinds of deficiency, so it is to be hoped that further experiment may give us more knowledge about their relative importance. It is worth noting that many African negroes regard with appalled horror European methods of caring for orphans; they seem as unnatural and immoral to them as polygamy or infant sacrifice do to us.

A quite different line of support for Hebb's theory comes from attempts to modify the ordinary perceptual mechanisms by living continuously in an abnormal environment. For instance, suppose one wears, all the time, a pair of spectacles with inverting lenses which turn the world upside down. At first this is very disturbing, but if one persists one becomes used to it and eventually sees the world normally. The time scale involved is a couple of weeks or so. This shows fairly clearly that we are not equipped by nature with a complete rigid mechanism for translating into perceptual experience the stimuli at our sense-organs. There must be some sort of self-adjusting mechanism which assures that when an object can be seen in a certain direction and touched by raising one's hand above one's head, then that direction is 'up'. The speed of the re-adjustment is a little startling by comparison with the time taken by a baby before it responds appropriately to visual stimuli, since one would have thought that reversing an already learned relationship would take longer. But the case may be reasonably thought of as similar to that of the red and black cards: it is easier to reverse a set of responses which are already present than it is to build up an entirely fresh set.

A last line of experiment which is very relevant to Hebb's theory, and started in his laboratory, is keeping people for long periods under conditions in which normal patterned stimulation does not occur. For instance, wearing translucent goggles to prevent any detailed vision, hearing a steady droning noise which masks out other sounds, and so on. When this is done for several days, efficiency falls off at a number of tasks, and there is some evidence that the normal compensating mechanisms cease to work so that perception is distorted. This looks as if the system of interconnected groups of cells needs to be kept functional if it is to survive. But there are other factors involved in this case, which we shall discuss later in the chapter when we consider Hebb's attitude to motivation.

## An Evaluation of Hebb's Theory

It must be said at once that Hebb has silenced the argument that some form of field function must occur in the brain because nothing else would fit the results. Most psychologists agree that his theory represents a way in which the brain might work. On the other hand, whether it *does* work in this way is quite another question. There is no positive evidence for it, and one's acceptance of the full weight of the theory rests rather on one's judgment about the future progress of physiology. Many people feel that the assumptions that the All-or-None Law holds for the cortex, and that the firing of two neighbouring cells lowers the threshold between them, are more probable than any field theory. But the latter is not to be ruled out completely. According to current views of the nervous system, the flow of each impulse along a nerve represents an electrical disturbance based on the presence of small oppositely charged particles inside and outside the nerve. Changes in the concentration of these particles may affect transmission along the nerve. Equally, at certain junctions in the nervous system chemical substances are known to be liberated which stimulate the next stage in the process. It is not quite inconceivable therefore that chemical concentrations in the cortex might be crucial features in its functioning: and these might be distributed in patterned fields which would not be disturbed by Lashley's experiments with conductors and insulators in the visual projection area. This is unlikely, but just conceivable; and it is also possible that the mechanism of the cortex is based on the All-or-None Law in some way which differs from that of Hebb. His theory therefore, despite its use of physiological language, is based essentially on Hull's method of making a guess and then trying to test it. It is open to the same objection that it takes insufficient notice of other alternative explanations: but it is probably better in this respect than Hullian theory is, because it is less detailed and consequently concerns itself with more general issues.

One point which should be borne in mind is that some sort of localization does definitely exist in the cortex. In man, for instance, injury at one particular spot on the side of the brain (the left side for right-handed men) is strongly associated with impairment of speech. Injury further up on the opposite side seems to produce difficulties in spatial orientation: the patient cannot draw maps and has trouble finding his way about. As many people know, injury to the front part of the cortex seems to make a man worse at 'planning ahead' and rather shallow in his personal relations, but since it sometimes makes him less tense and more tractable, there was at one time quite a fashion for deliberately producing such injury in psychiatric cases. Damage elsewhere is not usually reported as giving the same results.

These findings are not as clear-cut as the effects of removing one valve from a radio set. But they do show some localization of different functions. Animal experiments give roughly comparable results: for instance, animals injured in the front of the cortex are bad at problems which require them to observe something, wait for a while, and then act on their observation. Damage elsewhere in the brain does not affect this kind of problem more seriously than other problems. The connections within the cortex cannot be completely random. Hebb's view might perhaps take this into account by saying that although most functions are learned, there are factors which would make the learning tend to lie in particular regions. For instance, regions close to certain projection areas would obviously be involved in learning for those areas, and more remote connections might tend to develop in certain directions because more cells were available in those directions. At the same time, it is a more obvious explanation that certain mechanisms are built into the structure of the brain at birth and so are associated with particular regions.

These cautions and qualifications must not blind us to Hebb's great achievement. The importance of perceptual learning is clearly established and can never again be left out of account. A mechanism which, like Hebb's, is based on randomness, together with some device for capitalizing on the chance factor, has very considerable biological advantages. Not only will it be very resistent to damage, but it will also compensate to some extent for abnormalities in the sense-organs which supply it with information, and it will be capable of dealing with a variety of different environments rather than simply one particular type of situation. Remember the blind men who locate objects by sound: or for that matter, the business men who have a blood vessel burst in their brains and yet return to work within a surprisingly short time. It is all very well for human designers to make machines which will function only in one way, but if there is no mechanic to mend or rewire a device it is better for it to be self-adjusting and flexible.

Hebb's contribution therefore represents another instance of adaptation to the environment by random variation and selection. Species adjust by containing a variety of individuals, the best suited of which survive: behaviour adjusts by the appearance of a variety of actions, the best suited of which survive. If Hebb is right, the nervous system adjusts by possessing a variety of connections, the ones which are most used surviving. But this brings us to the question of reward and motivation.

## The Neurological Basis of Reward

In Hebb's system there is no mechanism ascribed to the Law of Effect. Cells are not joined because a reward is given, but simply because they fire in rapid succession. As in Guthrie's theory, reward merely changes the situation and so makes different cells fire. There is in fact no evidence about the effect of reward on the nervous system apart from one intriguing observation by Olds and Milner. The cortex lies, as has been said, like a dome or an umbrella, over the top of the spine, which bulges out into a number of structures through which the nervous messages pass on their way to and from the cortex. In this region under the umbrella there is a place into which Olds and Milner stuck an electrode and left it until the rat concerned had recovered from the operation. They then connected the electrode to a bar, so that if the bar was pressed the rat received a mild burst of current through the electrode. The rat itself learned to press the bar, and would do so quite happily although it received no food or other reward for its activity. As far as can be made out, stimulating this region of the nervous system has the same effect as giving a reward. Another place close by seems to act as a punishment, in so far as the rat will learn to turn off the stimulation. Drugs have different effects on the various centres, just as alcohol was mentioned in an earlier chapter to reduce the effects of punishment more than those of reward. More work is obviously needed on this topic, but as yet the implications are not completely clear.

So much, then, for the problem of the way in which a reward given to an active animal selects one of the activities in progress and makes it more likely to recur. But what makes the animal active in the first place? To Hull, the drive which produces activity results from some lack or need of the animal which stimulates it and so causes varied action. Hebb was critical of this emphasis on outside stimulation, which seems to make the nervous system purely passive. One can, for instance, detect electrical activity in groups of nerve cells detached altogether from the body, and it seems only reasonable to suppose that the brain has enough spontaneity to initiate action itself. Hebb later changed his views slightly, because of the experiments (already mentioned) on human beings in an abnormally monotonous environment. One of the most striking features of this research was that people were not willing to remain in these unstimulating conditions even though they were highly paid. This suggested that outside stimulation was indeed necessary to them, although not as a goad jabbing them into action, but rather simply as an end in itself. They were well-fed, not thirsty, and should have lacked for nothing: yet they sought activity when according to a simple Hullian view they ought to have become quite immobile.

This finding is not completely inconsistent with Hebb's earlier emphasis on the initiative of the organism. After all, it is the man himself who becomes dissatisfied with lack of stimulation and goes out to get it. But it does seem that the outside world plays a part in keeping the brain in trim, and that it would be impossible for a brain to go on thinking indefinitely if all its pathways from the senses were cut. As was said earlier in the chapter, there are secondary pathways which produce very general activity in the cortex when any stimulus arrives, and if these pathways are cut animals seem to go into a very stuporous and passive state. One may think therefore of each stimulus as having two roles, one to inform the cortex about the outside world, and the other to maintain the general level of activity which keeps the brain ready to respond adequately to events. When the level of stimulation drops, the nervous system becomes unresponsive even to the few things that do occur.

This point suggests that we should return to behaviour proper, and examine more carefully the evidence about drives and rewards.

# 7

# The Springs of Action

We have seen that the Law of Effect puts crucial importance on reward for selecting the correct action out of the varied activity of the animal. But what is the definition of a reward? From one point of view anything we do to an animal, which makes his immediately preceding action more probable, can be regarded as a reward. This definition is not as circular as it seems at first sight, because we are really saying that if giving substance X to one rat will teach it to press a bar, then we can also teach another rat to turn a wheel by giving substance X every time wheel-turning occurs. By labelling X as a ' reward' we indicate that it belongs to a general class of things which can operate the Law of Effect, and we are not simply saying that it produces learning because it produces learning. But it would obviously be still better if one could give an independent definition of rewards and relate them more closely to the biological background. For instance, it would be nice if we could say that giving a particular thing to an animal is rewarding when lack of that thing would imperil the survival of the animal or the species. If animals don't get food they die, and therefore food is a reward: if they do not find mates the species dies, and therefore a mate is a reward. It could easily be imagined that the ordinary process of evolution would rapidly eliminate animals who did not tend to repeat actions which secured food or mates.

Such a sweeping statement about the nature of rewards has therefore got its attractions, and it is worth considering the ways in which it could be extended to cover behaviour which at first sight is rather remote from primary biological needs. We do not give politicians a meal every time they make a speech: nor is close attention to a scientific laboratory quite the best way to secure a sexual partner. Admittedly business men tend to use meals as a technique in carrying out negotiations, but the intention seems to be to induce a general mood of bonhomie rather than to reward tendencies towards a favourable settlement. As a result of this apparent absence of primary reward in human behaviour, there was in Edwardian times a tendency to list motives or instincts on a rather generous scale, and to suppose that rewards such as power or fame could not be reduced to more primary biological needs. But the danger of this approach is that it becomes in the end meaningless to consider motives at all, because wherever a kind of behaviour can be distinguished one can promptly label it with a fresh motive. If a man digs his garden, this may be a horticultural instinct, and if he goes for a stroll this is a stroll-going instinct. If on the other hand one tries to relate either of these activities to some more general motive, why should not that in turn be related to primary needs? The answer, we may as well say at once, is that the primary needs alone are not adequate to explain all the experimental evidence. But it is interesting to see how far one can get with their aid alone, and it is also an object lesson in the fact that a plausible theory of behaviour is not necessarily true.

Clinical experience of mental illness has led many psychiatrists to emphasize the role of the primary needs, and especially that of sex, in the organization of adult behaviour. Some of them would argue that all neurosis arises from a disorder in sexual adjustment and persists until appropriate satisfaction is obtained: if not directly, then in some sublimated form such as science or art whose energy is supposed to be derived from the primary need. This view has quite important consequences for treatment. For instance, if a bachelor business man suffers from fits of extravagant anxiety with palpitations, sweating, and so on, is it adequate to refer him to a good industrial consultant to have his business organized on a more efficient and secure basis? Or ought one rather to examine why he cares so much about the future of an abstract organization, and try to divert his interests into the domestic channels which he lacks?

## The Possibilities of Indirect Reward

The fact which makes it conceivable that all behaviour may ultimately be based on primary needs is the possibility of associating reward with the situation in which it is given. If a stimulus is present during reward, that stimulus takes on some of the properties of reward. For example, suppose one teaches rats to press a lever by connecting the lever to a machine which delivers a food pellet for each pressure. If the machine makes a loud click every time it operates, the rat will, when the supply of pellets is exhausted, go on pressing the bar much longer than it will if the machine is completely silent. The click itself is rewarding. In the same way an animal will run through a maze more willingly to an empty box in which it has been fed than it will to a completely strange box. In a more complicated vein, one can train monkeys to operate a slot machine which gives them a grape every time they insert a token: and one can then teach them to do some other action by giving them a token each time they do the correct thing. The token or the empty food box now 'mean' food and act in the same way to reinforce learning.

Even in the action of primary reward, the stimulation of the senses involved is important and it is not simply the meeting of the need, the 'consummatory act' mentioned in Chapter II, which acts as a reward. If we take an animal which has had the canal from its mouth to its stomach operated upon, it is possible to feed it and to remove the food before it reaches the stomach. No need is satisfied, and the animal has merely received the sensory stimulation it would normally get from eating. Yet it will learn to do things for the sake of this stimulation. Incidentally, it will also learn for the sake of food which is placed directly into its stomach without passing its mouth, but not so well as it will for a more conventional reward. Similar points can be made without using operated animals: a male rat will learn a particular response in order simply to reach a female even though it is not allowed to reach the full consummatory act. And rats will learn a maze in order to receive saccharin, which is not in fact nutritive and so does not meet a need. It is not clear in the cases mentioned how far the stimuli concerned are innately able to act as rewards, and how far they do so because they have in the past been present during the satisfaction of a need. This point is still being investigated: but in any event it is clear that simply receiving certain kinds of stimulation may act as a reward, and that a given stimulus may achieve this status by learning.

Now human beings have a long childhood in which they require to have their physical needs met by their elders. Normally speaking, a baby's mother is present whenever he is fed, removed from discomfort, or satisfied in any other way. It is likely therefore that the appearance of his mother will itself become rewarding for him, and that he will do things which result in her appearance and in her giving him attention. He is also likely to be more rewarded by her appearance when she is disposed to minister to him than when she is cross with him: and as the years go by other people also will act as rewards in so far as they share common characteristics with her. When this stage is reached, if he finds that concentration on his school work produces smiles of approval from his mother and his teacher, he will find those smiles rewarding even though they are not immediately and inevitably backed up by bars of chocolate.

This then is a possible mechanism by which behaviour having no apparent biological advantage could be learned: the primary reward might be replaced by more generalized social approval, but the ultimate source of the behaviour would be the link between the child and those who cared for him in infancy. As a result, of course, it would be difficult to teach such behaviour to a child who has never had the opportunity of learning the association between reward and the mother's approval. It is dangerous to expect somebody from a really bad home to learn his lessons in order to obtain friendship and sympathy from the teacher. He first has to learn the meaning of the various signs of interest and approval which one person can give to another, and if one omits that stage one may well be unsuccessful in training him. But, as we said earlier, this factor is at the moment combined to an unknown extent with lack of a suitable basis of experience with which to assimilate new learning. Further study is needed.

One other aspect of indirect reward ought to be mentioned again at this point, and that is the importance of anxiety. The experiments in which animals avoid punishment show that some process must be postulated inside the animal if the Law of Effect is to be kept intact; and once it is admitted that particular situations may put the organism into an unpleasant state so that it strives to escape from them, there is a plausible explanation available for many kinds of persistent but apparently useless behaviour. The politician, the scientist, or the business man may be regarded as avoiding anxiety by their activities, rather than seeking social approval. In either case the persistence of their behaviour will depend upon their early upbringing, but the advantage of anxiety from the point of view of the upholder of the importance of physical needs, is that it can explain the very long persistence of actions which have not been reinforced. So far as casual observation of human life is concerned, it might well be possible to account for all behaviour in these relatively simple terms. But experiment forces one to conclude that the physical needs are not the only factors in motivation, and it is worth following in some detail the line of argument which has established this.

## On Not Doing the Same Thing Twice

If we put a rat in a maze shaped like a T, it has two choices. It can turn right or left. If on one occasion we give it food for turning right, we might expect it to repeat that action next time it enters the maze. In fact it is a fairly safe prediction that it will not: it will turn the opposite way. This seems quite contrary to the Law of Effect, although actually it is still true that over a long series of

168

trials the rewarded response will grow more frequent. But there is a strong tendency not to repeat a response on two immediately successive occasions, and the effect of reward only functions in the context of this other effect. It immediately strikes one that the rat is 'curious' or 'exploring', but simpler explanations must be considered first.

The first explanation given for this alternation of response was that it was due to the 'inhibitory' or fatiguing effect of making each response. In Hull's theory, the inhibition resulting from reaction is necessary to eliminate the responses which are not followed by reward. The successful response is the only one to be strengthened to resist this inhibition, and so it is the one which survives. Now it is reasonable, if such inhibition occurs, that the rat should tend to alternate between two possible choices. If he did not, one response would become more and more inhibited.

This explanation seems satisfactory, and at first sight has little to do with the nature of reward. But suppose now that the rats are put in a cross-shaped maze, and started towards the cross-roads alternately from the North and the South. If they turn right on their first trial, they ought to have accumulated inhibition of that response and so to turn left on the next run. However, as they are now coming from the opposite direction, that response would take them to the same place. In fact they turn right again and explore the fourth arm of the maze. It is as though a man who has for pleasure taken a walk down one road is offered his choice of a car-ride down the same road or another walk in a fresh direction. Whatever the man might choose, the rat seems to prefer a new place rather than a new kind of response. So a straightforward theory of inhibition, assuming that process to resemble fatigue, will not do.

One might perhaps modify the theory so as to think of the inhibition as applying, not to any external action, but to some event in the brain which results from the stimuli associated with the place the rat is observing. It might be, for instance, that the cluster of nerve cells suggested by Hebb would fire for one place and then be reluctant to fire again. Accordingly, when the rat looked from side to side at the cross-roads, it would experience more activity in its brain from the new path than it would from the old one, and it would set off along the new one. This theory is not completely satisfactory, because of another experiment.

In this case the rat had the choice of two paths; animals were observed under conditions in which both paths led to different places, and under another condition in which they both led to the same place. The rats tended to alternate more markedly when they would get to a different place by doing so. This experiment, like the others, shows that the animal is not very much affected by the response as opposed to the situation which will result from the response: but it also shows that a novel situation attracts the animal even when it is not now present to the senses, because the rat could not see from the cross-roads what was at the end of the paths. Just as a man can consider the direction of his walk without at that moment seeing the places which lie at the end of each road, so also can the rat. And it chooses the place not recently seen.

Again one can modify the theory, by supposing that the inhibited event within the brain is not a result of stimulation but rather part of the 'map-within-the-head' built up by experience. Put in human terms, after one has just seen a place one is reluctant to think about it, and so less likely to respond to the path which leads to it; using concepts from the last two chapters, the firing of a group of cells by direct stimulation makes it difficult to use them just afterwards as part of a chain producing $r_g$ and so inducing action.

By this stage, the theory has become rather remote from its first form. But a last experiment should be mentioned because it almost compels us to drop any inhibitory idea altogether, and to consider novelty of a situation as a quality which increases the responsiveness of the animal – rather than familiarity a quality which decreases it. In this experiment the rat runs up to a T junction and looks at two paths, one black and one white. Glass doors stop him from going down either, so he does not make any response to one rather than the other. Presumably he has aroused the processes in his brain which correspond to black and those which correspond to white, and so both should be equally inhibited. He is then put in the maze again, without the glass partitions there, but with both paths black. He tends to enter the one which was formerly white. The neatness of this experiment is that the two paths ought to be equal, were it not for the fact that one of them used to be different. Blackness in itself should not attract the animal to one arm rather than the other: but change does. At this point it seems easier to cease thinking of a fatigue-like mechanism stopping brain processes from occurring, and to think rather of a positive tendency for the animal to select novel situations and examine them. Not everybody would agree with this judgment, and there is much experimentation still proceeding on the matter: but there are also a number of studies on the use of novel stimuli as a reward, and these we ought now to consider.

## Exploration of the World as a Motive

When one places a rat in a maze, it promptly wanders about, entering each of the alleys. This tendency to explore is sometimes stronger than the direct satisfaction of the animal's needs. For instance, even a hungry rat will explore a strange place although there is food in plain sight. This is perhaps biologically useful, since it means that the animal is not easily enticed by food into dangerous situations. But it does not fit into a view of motivation which holds that basic rewards are things which supply direct needs of the animal. Rather it seems that the chance to see, smell and touch unusual situations is attractive to the rat just as food is.

The attraction varies with the extent to which the situation is really unfamiliar. For example, one can measure the interest aroused in a rat by an object in the following way. A cage or other space which the animal knows well can be divided up into several areas, and an observer can keep count of the amount of time spent by a rat in each area. If now a strange object is placed in one of the areas, the rat will spend longer in that area: the inference seems a fair one that he is examining the object. If several strange objects are put in on one day, and then one of them is changed on a second day leaving the others as they were, it is the new object which will be examined. The rat tries to get more of the unusual stimuli.

This tendency to approach strange objects appears primarily in laboratory rats, which have been bred for many generations for tameness. Wild rats explore if they find themselves in completely strange surroundings but keep carefully away from some odd object placed in an otherwise familiar place. If this were not so, they would be much easier to trap and poison. This kind of difference between closely related animals emphasizes the way in which the behaviour of a breed reflects the environment in which that breed lives: but it still disagrees with the simple view that reward is the end of a physical deprivation.

The attractiveness of novel objects does not by itself show that they possess all the characteristics of, say, food or drink rewards. The more usual rewards not only attract an animal when they are shown to him, but also cause him to repeat any action which they follow. It is particularly interesting therefore that exploration can act to produce learning, just as food will. If for example a rat is put in a simple T maze, one arm of which is a blind alley while the other leads to a bigger and more complicated maze, the animal will learn to take the path which gives it a chance to explore. Equally a monkey will learn to open a window which allows him to look out at the varied activity going on in the laboratory: there is an apocryphal story that a certain psychologist once left a monkey alone in a room and tried to observe the animal's activity through a spy-hole. All he could see was a large eye, since the monkey was trying to observe him.

The exploration of the space around the animal is in fact only one of a general class of rewards, arising from the manipulation of the surroundings. A rat confined in a cage with a lever will learn to press the lever if by so doing he turns on a weak light: just as young children often delight in playing with electric light switches. Doing something which produces a change in the world acts as a reward. Of course, it might conceivably be argued that this effect is due to previous association with a primary reward, but some experimenters have tried to eliminate this factor by rearing animals under closely controlled conditions. For instance, one can bring up kittens by hand, making sure that they never have to explore or manipulate in order to get food. Then one can try them out in a T maze which has a blind alley and an alley containing objects such as a rolled ball of newspaper. As anybody who knows kittens might suspect, they learn to choose the alley which gives them something to play with. The importance of the experiment is that it argues against this characteristic of kittens being something they have learned from association with food or drink. They just like playing.

## Stimulus Hunger and the Acquisition of Knowledge

We see therefore that the simple generalization, that reward is the meeting of a physiological deficit, will not do. Hunger, thirst, and sex could be regarded as producing each its appropriate stimulus, removal of which acts as a reward. But the rat which turns on a light is positively creating a stimulus for itself. It cannot be regarded as attempting to remove an irksome irritation which is disturbing its placidity. Animals therefore do not become active only when disturbed, and we must look further for the biological advantages of manipulation and exploration.

On Hebb's view, a good deal of learning of a rather general type is needed to build up the mechanisms which permit later specific learning. Objects have to be seen with various parts of the eye, and from various angles, so that the animal or man concerned can learn the equivalence of sensory impressions which are obtained in various ways. Such learning must take place during manipulation, since, as we have seen, young animals who are deprived of the chance to explore a varied environment grow up deficient in it. Quite apart from this general learning, the specific knowledge of particular situations is also acquired by exploration. In

173

Chapter IV we discussed the phenomenon of 'latent learning', in which a rat who is merely left in a maze without reward gains a knowledge of the maze which appears in later performance. The exploration of an empty maze is not mere wandering about; it builds up inside the animal a set of interconnected events corresponding to the structure of the maze. To Hull these events are fractional responses which can lead to $r_g$; to Tolman they are sign-gestalt-expectancies or, as we have paraphrased his view, a 'map-inside-the-head'. To Hebb the symbolic events, corresponding to the outer world, are best described as cell-assemblies. But whatever the label given to them, the pressure of the evidence makes it clear that they exist and that they are built up during exploration and manipulation.

It is dangerous to leap too blithely from the rat sniffing his way into a strange alley, to the scientist observing the way in which dew forms in some places rather than in others. Nevertheless at the very least one can say that human beings differ from rats in the direction of increased complication and independence of the momentary situation. If even rats have a tendency to observe events independently of physical need, and to build up a model of the world as the result of that observation, it seems plausible that human beings are even less likely to base all their activity on primary needs. This, of course, does not mean that interference with primary needs is not a potent source of mental disorder. In our society the most likely need to be frustrated in this way is probably sex, but there is no other obvious reason why that particular drive should hold a special place in the production of abnormal behaviour. Some psychiatrists have of course pointed out in the past that it seems unnecessary to seek for sexual disturbances to explain breakdowns in soldiers under the strain of battle, where the conflicts arise from a different cause. People living in some other kinds of society seem to have much less trouble with sex than we do: perhaps they are troubled by other drives instead.

Even though it is clear that the desire to explore the world and expose oneself to novel stimuli is not simply derived from the primary drives, there remains the possibility that a state of hunger, thirst, or sexual need might interact with curiosity. It might well be that a hungry artist constructs new and stimulating visual patterns more vigorously because of his hunger, even though the roots of his art lie in a drive to explore visual experience and not in any primary need. Certainly in the case of animals an increase in the intensity of a need does produce increased exploration. A hungry rat moves about its surroundings more than one which is satisfied. Some experimenters have claimed that the size of the effect produced by novel stimuli depends on the amount of primary drive present: putting a rat in a novel situation produces a great deal of exploration *if* the rat is hungry. This kind of evidence certainly supports the idea that primary needs supply energy to other kinds of activity.

Activity alone, however, is not a very satisfactory measure: as we said earlier, the important thing about exploration is not only that the animal pushes its nose into strange places, but that it learns about the places in the process. We know that a rat which has eaten as much as it wants can be put into a maze, that it will simply explore the maze without special notice of food placed in one part, and that if it is then made hungry and replaced in the maze it will go very rapidly to the food. Is this latent learning increased by hunger or thirst? Obviously a hungry rat would learn the position of the food very rapidly: but this is unfair because the reward value of the food is greater for such an animal. But if we make a rat thirsty, let it explore a maze containing food, and then make it hungry before testing its knowledge of the maze, it shows less learning than a completely satisfied animal would. The same thing applies the other way round: a hungry animal is bad at learning the position of water. So it seems that a strong specific need may increase the activity of the animal, but actually make it hard for it to learn in the generalized way which we have found to be so important. If the analogy from animal to man holds, a person who is driven by some basic need may well apply himself more violently to academic learning: but will only succeed in learning those things which are directly or indirectly related to his need. One must remain rather sceptical therefore about the possibility of a physical need, such as sex, lending vigour to the manipulation of general conceptual experience, although there is the evidence of the increased activity of animals in a state of need and some interrelationship may therefore exist.

## Conclusions on the Nature of Motives

The simple idea that reward consists of the removal of unpleasant stimulation, based on physical need, is clearly too simple. In the case of exploration, animals strive to secure stimulation and increase it: and this tendency is not based on a physical need. It is therefore necessary to fall back on the almost circular definition used at the beginning of the chapter, that a reward is something which produces learning. Such a definition has its merits, as was said when it was first introduced, and it is not inconsistent with the broad biological picture. In some species very detailed modes of behaviour are inborne in the individual animal: although some of the details of bird-song are learnt, the general type of song is shown even by birds brought up away from their parents. When one interferes with such innate behaviour, as for instance by feeding a predatory species by hand, the tendency to perform the unused actions seems almost to become a drive, and they emerge where there is no necessity for them to be used to rectify the simple physical need. Animals which show courtship rituals will not mate without going through the ritual. So we must suppose that particular kinds of behaviour have been built in by evolution, because they are on the whole adaptive, even though they are not direct acquisitions of something which is physically lacking. The way in which they are built in is one which ensures that they will occur despite minor deviations of the environment, that is, the animal will vary its actions persistently until they can occur. Beyond this it seems unrealistic to go on classifying rewards, since they do not obey any general rule that has yet been put forward.

We need not therefore regard the more complex and subtle of human pleasures as necessarily based on the primary needs. All the same, in a species which learns so readily we ought to beware of supposing that any motive is self-supporting, and independent of more basic ones unless we have definite evidence that it is. Curiosity and exploration seem so widespread amongst mammals that it is likely that human eagerness to experience a variety of sensations and to build complex models of the world are primary motives. Art and science need not necessarily rest solely on hunger or sex. But beyond this we should not go in calling our desires natural and innate. Our childhood is so long, and offers so many opportunities for us to learn that particular kinds of behaviour are associated with primary reward, that we would expect to grow up with a battery of secondary rewards which have been learned to the point where we are lost without them. It is not surprising that in one society people compete and attempt to dominate each other, while in another they co-operate and conform. The men in each have learned the connection between their own actions and basic rewards. Thus members of the same species may show widely different motives depending on their training.

# 8

# The Next Step

We have now seen a fair sample of the activities of behaviour theorists during the half-century since Watson first launched them on their way. A lot has been left out, but the time has now come to look back over the whole field and try to draw some conclusions.

In the first place, it certainly seems to have been worth while to try experiments on behaviour. A large number of facts have emerged, some surprising, and some in accordance with the traditional wisdom of experienced men. Indeed, it can hardly have escaped the reader that these experimental results should produce no radical change in the normal practice of sensitive people when dealing with their fellows. The dangers of punishment (and its occasional advantages), the importance for children of variety of experience and secure fundamental relationships, or the fact that physical satisfactions do not exhaust human desires, need not surprise us too greatly; although our insight into each of these principles should have been improved by the results given in earlier pages. But of course many people do require convincing of the validity of such principles, even though other people may find them obvious. The merit of objective study of behaviour is that it provides a means of testing intuitive knowledge and sorting the true from the false; not that it should necessarily provide some quite different and previously unheard of method of dealing with people. One of the objections sometimes raised to the study of behaviour is that it may upset traditional ideas about moral and correct action: but if one really believes in such ideas one should expect them to be confirmed by experiment, and ought to welcome the chance of gaining objective support as an aid in convincing others. The other objection, that no general principles can be established about behaviour because it is too variable, has clearly been overthrown. Facts in profusion have been discovered.

A second point is that these facts fit reasonably well into a general evolutionary picture. Species adapt to their environment by producing various different individuals, of whom the best suited survive: on a higher level, the behaviour of one individual can be adapted to his circumstances by a mechanism which makes him vary his activity until he reaches a certain state or goal. On a higher level still, achievement of a goal in a particular way can make that way of behaving more common in future, speeding up the process of adaptation even further: and lastly, the animal can develop within itself a model of the outer world on which various actions can be tried out and only the successful act put into practice. When this last stage is reached, behaviour can be immediately adaptive to the particular circumstances of the individual animal, and the slow process of the evolution of species has been made almost instantaneous. This stage certainly appears to some extent in rats and monkeys, although it is of course far more effective and far-ranging in men. But the continuity is unbroken, and the whole process can be seen as one which takes advantage of random variation to produce novel adjustments to strange and unfamiliar situations.

Paralleling the use of varying behaviour to secure adaptation, there is some evidence for a partially random arrangement of the brain, which then becomes organized in particular ways dependent on the experience of the individual animal. Such a method of producing a mechanism makes it far more resistant to damage, and able to cope with more peculiar environments, than it would be if the detailed inter-connections of the brain were laid down at birth. In variability, in plasticity, in the very factors which have made some people suspicious of the attempt to study behaviour scientifically, there are definite advantages.

Perhaps the key step in the production of this view of behaviour was the realization by several people, about 1930, that an ordinary scientific analysis in terms of cause and effect can be applied to purposive activity. Traditionally, there has been an opposition between teleological explanations ('that man is walking along the road in order to buy some bread in the village') and causal ones ('that man is falling in the lake because he was pushed'). The teleological type of explanation was thought to involve the action of a future event upon the present, and so to conflict with ordinary scientific ideas. But in the case of purposive animal behaviour, the cause need not be the future event, but merely some present event within the animal's nervous system. It is not the buying of bread, which is an event still in the future, that makes a man walk to the village. Rather it is his need of bread, which is an event in the present. Although this distinction is so simple, it seems to have been missed in many earlier discussions of purpose. Once it has been made, we can easily see how the normal process of evolution could produce animals which would, in a state of need, 'switch on' restless behaviour and keep varying it until 'switched off' by a reward. The sequence of cause and effect runs in the normal direction and the explanation is no different from any other scientific one.

Despite the general success of the experimental attack on behaviour, there are a number of criticisms which can be made of the results so far obtained: and these are important because they suggest the lines on which future development is likely to run.

## The Neglect of Natural Behaviour

Almost all the research has been concentrated upon a few species and predominantly upon the rat. That animal has been bred for laboratory convenience, and is different even from wild rats, as we saw in the last chapter. It is therefore extremely dangerous to put forward principles purporting to be general ones applying to all behaviour, on the basis of that single type of animal. Furthermore, even the rat's activity has been studied almost entirely from the point of view of theoretical approaches to learning: innate behaviour has hardly been considered, nor have many people looked at the rat without preconceptions. It is hard to see how we could have waited forty years without an analysis of exploration had this not been so.

Both these weaknesses, the neglect of other species and of innate behaviour, are likely to be countered by increased contact between psychologists and zoologists. While the former have been turning from men to the study of learning in simpler animals, their colleagues have been turning from the anatomy and physiology of animals to the study of behaviour. Zoologists specializing in this field are often called 'ethologists', and they tend to study innate behaviour rather more than the mechanisms of learning. They also tend to start the study of an animal by observing it in its natural surroundings, proceeding to experiment at a later stage to clarify the mechanism of some piece of behaviour. For example, if it is noted that a female of a certain species usually responds to a sideways-jumping movement of the male, the experimenter may show to the female a jumping model bearing little other resemblance to the male, and thus find out whether the movement itself is the stimulus, or whether some other feature of the male is important. A number of results from ethological researches were mentioned in Chapter II, and there is no doubt that this rather different emphasis will have a salutary effect on future theories of behaviour. It is already true that attitudes to 'drive' and 'reward' have been changed by ethology. As we saw in the last chapter, the study of instinctive behaviour shows that quite complex actions may be necessary to the animal just as primary physical needs are: a fact which a psychologist studying rats in mazes might never have discovered.

## Premature Formalization

Another besetting weakness of behaviour theory is that it has tended to rush into comprehensive and detailed theoretical statements at too early a stage. Watson's early account of conditioning, as based simply on the occurrence of a stimulus and response at the same time, was an example of this: but the clearest case is probably that of the Law of Effect in its elaborate form as put forward by Hull. Although it is true that animals do, in general, whatever they are rewarded for doing, it does not seem that a simple stamping-in of stimulus-response connections by subsequent reward is the one and only basic principle of learning. Experiments force us to conclude that even rats form inside their heads models of the outside world (chains of fractional anticipatory responses); and that when the model contains a part which corresponds to something which would be a reward for the animal at that time (an $r_g$), the actions which lead to the reward are translated into overt activity. Many, perhaps most, psychologists now seem to think that the building up of the model requires little or no reward. It was therefore premature for Hull to set up a highly complex and detailed theory which treated reward as an essential condition of learning. Furthermore, the number of details in his theory was very much the same as the number of facts which he was trying to explain, and the theory did not therefore condense evidence into a simple statement: which most people would think a theory ought to do.

There are various consequences of this criticism. On the one hand, there is the increased enthusiasm for Skinner's approach, an enthusiasm which we mentioned in Chapter V. So long as this implies that psychologists will confine themselves purely to stating what they observe, it is a genuine improvement on Hull's approach. But unfortunately one cannot confine oneself in this way for ever: all of us want to give a scientific account of behaviour in complex situations where more is involved than the frequency of some simple action. It is possible to make predictions in such situations on the basis of experiments carried out under simpler conditions: but we then often have a choice between various features of the complex situation, each of which might correspond to some feature of the simple one. We must therefore make theoretical assumptions in applying the results of the simple case, and as the followers of Skinner have no rules for doing this with greater caution than the Hullians, there is a danger that they may make just as rash pronouncements. The present writer would regard Skinner's views of language as an example of the dangers in this approach.

Another way of facing the problem is the use of more sophisticated mathematics. During the Fifties, various theories have been set up in mathematical form, so that one can compare the number of predictions with the number of assumptions and thus confirm that the theory is serving a useful purpose. The two most notable theories of this kind are those of Estes, and of Bush and Nosteller. Roughly speaking, the first of these is a sophisticated version of Guthrie's theory mentioned in Chapter II, while Bush and Mosteller's is a superior form of Hull's theory. That is, Estes treats the amount learned at any instant as affected solely by the frequency with which the learned event has occurred: while Bush and Mosteller treat it as the result of positive learning from correct actions minus a negative tendency opposing the repetition of any response. Oddly enough, when the two theories are applied to similar situations they give rather similar equations, so that as usual it is hard to test one theory in contrast to the other.

One of the merits of Estes' theory is that it gives an explanation of an odd fact about human and animal behaviour. Suppose you play the well-known guessing game with a child, of putting a sweet in one of your own clenched fists, then holding out both fists and asking him to guess which hand has the sweet in it. Unless you give the secret away somehow he will guess right on about half his attempts. But now suppose that you change the sweet occasionally from hand to hand, but on the average keep it in the right hand three times out of four and in the left hand only once out of four. Most children (and adults for that matter) will tend after a while to guess the right hand three times as often as they do the left. But this is an inefficient thing to do. The chance of their guessing the right hand at the same time as you actually put the sweet in it is only $\frac{3}{4} \times \frac{3}{4}$, that is, nine times out of sixteen. In addition they will get the sweet in the left hand once out of sixteen tries; so in all they will win ten times out of sixteen. They would have done better to stick rigidly to the right hand, when they would of course have won twelve times out of sixteen.

This fact is particularly interesting because it shows that the Law of Effect does not always result in the best possible behaviour from the animal's point of view. Estes explains it by saying that every time a correct guess occurs a proportion of the stimuli which are present, but which are not yet attached to any response, become attached to that guess. The probability of the guess varies with the number of stimuli tending to produce it; and this can be shown by fairly simple algebra to lead to a balance in which even the less useful guess does occur on a certain proportion of trials. Incidentally, as there will, at the beginning of the experiment, be more unattached stimuli about, learning should be more rapid then than it will later, a prediction which is very often true. The idea that the stimuli present are 'sampled', and only some of them get learned, is particularly interesting because of cybernetic ideas which we will mention later in the chapter. If one accepts Estes' mathematics, the results of a large number of experiments in various laboratories agree that the proportion of stimuli actually present which are learned on any one trial is about a twentieth; a solemn thought.

Bush and Mosteller, like Estes, can predict the fact that people and animals do not consistently choose that action which pays off most frequently: because their theory includes a tendency not to repeat actions, rather like Hull's reactive inhibition. In the special case of the guessing game, the equations derived from the two theories become remarkably similar. But in addition Bush and Mosteller can handle other cases such as the rate at which a single action will occur if it is always followed by reward. As in Estes' account of the guessing game, the action is likely to become more frequent very markedly at first, and then only to increase more slowly. Bush and Mosteller attempt to fit the exact shape of the learning curves in such situations, and in others, and their theory rests largely on the close resemblance between the theoretical curves and the ones actually found in experiments. The basic logic is the same as in Hull's 'guess-and-check' approach to scientific method; but instead of making checks by predicting an odd fact like the rise in efficiency of memory during the first minute or two after learning has stopped, Bush and Mosteller rely on the exact correspondence between the speed and limits of learning worked out theoretically and those observed experimentally. It is the exact numbers which are important to them, and not merely rough observations that one group of animals performs better than another.

These mathematical models for behaviour are undoubtedly superior versions of the 'guess-and-check' approach, because the checks involve more measurements than there are assumptions in the theory. As we saw in Chapter V, Hull had an unfortunate tendency to have as many assumptions as he did actual observations. It is likely that more theories of this mathematical type will appear in the future. Nevertheless, the present writer is not completely happy about this development. In the last chapter we discussed some of the difficulties of an 'inhibitory' theory, and made it clear that some of the crude observations made of animal behaviour cast great doubt upon the reality of any such inhibition. Yet Bush and Mosteller used it (before the contrary evidence had reached the stage recounted in the last chapter) in their analysis of the detailed numerical performance of rats learning to press a bar. Again, a striking result of statistical theory is the explanation of the guessing game. But recent results suggest that, in man, these results are due to the dissatisfaction which people normally feel at accepting something less than complete success. If it is made plain to the guessers that they cannot win every time, because there is a random element in the occurrence of the sweet in either hand, then they may distribute their guesses in a different way. Only when they are trying to find a pattern in the movement of the sweet will they match the guesses to the actual frequency of appearances of the sweet on one side and the other. If then the detailed results hold true only when the task is being performed in one particular fashion can we really place much trust in the intricate mathematical model which is justified by those detailed, results? As we concluded when discussing Hull's approach, it is better to settle the general principles of behaviour before going into too much detailed elaboration of a set of principles that may be false. Alternative theories also should be set up, rather than putting forward one guess alone. But if the danger of premature formalization is really avoided, there is a good deal of merit in the attempt to bring mathematics more closely into psychological theory. It is impossible in mathematical reasoning to make false inferences and rely upon concealed assumptions to such an extent as theories of behaviour have done in the past. The increased rigour of mathematics is certainly a gain, provided it is based on experimental work of comparable rigour and scope.

## The Absence of Physiology

Another weakness in most of the approaches previously discussed (not of course that of Hebb) is the lack of any connection with physiology. There has been no attempt to link concepts such as anxiety or $r_g$ with nervous mechanisms: and this is clearly a short-sighted way to study behaviour. One might as well study the behaviour of motor-cars completely from the outside, ignoring the nature of the engine or the steering-gear. It is highly probable that important features of behaviour will be found to depend upon the nature of the nervous system, and by leaving physiology out of account we cut ourselves off from an important source of information.

At the same time, the gulf between studies of the brain and studies of behaviour has impoverished physiology itself. Most of the people who study the nervous system are not familiar with the literature on behaviour, and this undoubtedly hampers their own work. For example, we have seen that the Pavlovian conditioned reflex is not to be interpreted too lightly as being the attachment of a response to a stimulus simply because it happens at about the same time. It is likely that the bell becomes a stimulus for salivation because the food is a reward as well as being the natural stimulus for mouth-watering. The whole situation is far more complicated than Pavlov or Watson thought. Yet respectable physiologists are still to be found constructing possible nervous mechanisms which might behave in the way Edwardian students of behaviour thought their animals behaved. Text-books of physiology still give Pavlov's interpretation of his results as though it were unquestioned, and allow no place for the effect of rewards, although for thirty years the inadequacy of 'association by contiguity' has been widely accepted by psychologists. It can hardly be doubted that this failure of communication between specialists in the two fields must be overcome if the brain is to be properly understood. There is no point at all in producing a theory of the brain which would make it behave quite differently from the way real animals behave.

The techniques used by psychologists can also be of value in the experimental work of physiologists. It very often arises that the properties of a drug or the functions of a part of the nervous system require study, and in such a case the physiologist may devise some behavioural experiment by the light of nature. He might, for instance, require the animal to learn not to eat when a certain stimulus is present, on pain of an electric shock: and then see whether a drugged animal still behaves correctly. But we have seen that learning based on avoidance of punishment is quite different from that based on reward – it is more resistant to extinction, shows a more rapid decay as the animal is removed to a different situation, is less attached to particular responses and more to the situation, and so on. If a drug causes feeding to reappear in an avoidance situation it may be because of reduction in the anxiety response, increase in the hunger drive, change in the stimulus situation, or any one of various other possibilities. To draw any valid conclusion about the drug, it is necessary to analyse the behaviour more carefully in various situations, and not to leap to the conclusion that, say, the drug causes forgetting because a learned avoidance of eating is lost under its influence. The techniques of psychologists can therefore be of value in the research of physiologists as well as in their theorizing.

There are hopeful signs that a bridge is being built between the two sciences, and that in future we shall see less of the disembodied behaviour theories of the past. Hebb's influence has been salutary in this respect, and in many centres of research the effects of brain injuries and of drugs are being studied using the most sophisticated techniques of psychologists. The most frequently used methods are those of Skinner, and there is still perhaps a need for studies of the more complicated insightful or '$r_g$ mediated' kinds of behaviour in relation to drugs and the brain. But at least there is now some contact of physiologists with psychologists, and there is much to be hoped from it in the years to come.

## The Weakness of Describing Unobservables

Perhaps the worst weakness of behaviour theory is its method of dealing with events inside the brain. One by one the simple theories, which treated only observed responses, have been eliminated. It is almost universally admitted now that even the behaviour of rats requires us to think of mechanisms operating purely inside their brains, and revealing themselves only indirectly in action. To mention some of the facts again: a rat can be taught to run along a path, then given a shock at the far end, and when placed at the entrance will be more reluctant to run. A rat can be taught two paths on separate occasions, and will recombine them to secure a new goal when the situation demands it. A man who is faced with a complex mass of stimuli and taught to respond to the presence of a particular signal will find it easier to reverse his behaviour and respond to the absence of that signal than he will to start responding to some new and quite different stimulus. (Similar behaviour has been shown in rats by D. H. Lawrence.) *

* No, a different one.

188

Experiments of this type can only be explained by internal, un-observed, mediating responses. In the first case, the entrance to the path must give rise to some response which normally occurs at the far end of the path, and this in turn produces the response to shock. In the second case, the entrance to one path must produce internal responses corresponding to the far end of that path and also to the start of the next, and so to the far end of the next path and to the goal. In the third case, the crucial stimulus must have been linked to some event within the brain which in turn can be attached to overt actions more readily than a new stimulus can be linked to any response of the organism.

The question then arises, how should we speak of these internal responses? The simplest way, and that which is still probably the one favoured by the majority of workers in the area, is to regard them as responses just like those we observe directly, obeying the same rules, and called simply 'responses' with perhaps some special symbol (like $r_g$) to show that one infers them rather than observes them. The advantage of this technique is that the meaning of any theoretical statement should be clear to all concerned. If like Tolman we speak of expectancies or readinesses, not all our listeners will understand quite what we mean.

But there are dangers in this approach as well as the advantage of clarity. Because we use the same word both for observed and for unobserved events, we may be under constant pressure to identify the $r_g$ as an action of the muscles and glands when there is no evidence against its being simply the firing of a nerve cell far within the nervous system. There are cases on record in which behaviour theorists have suggested that the 'observing responses' necessary to explain Lawrence's experiment are simply orienta-tions of the head and eyes and while this is not positively known to be untrue, it is surely a complete speculation on present evidence. There seems to be an echo here of Watson's belief that thinking consisted of faint twitches of the larynx and the speech muscles: psychologists are still keen to believe a particular fact because it will simplify their task if it is true.

Perhaps more serious is the fact that we cannot regard the internal mediating responses as obeying the same rules as overt ones do. Deutsch's point will be remembered, that the $r_g$ corresponding to drinking cannot be reinforced by a reward of food. If it were, a thirsty rat would go to the place where it was fed, whereas of course, it goes only to the place where it found water. Overt actions can be reinforced by any reward, but $r_g$ only by the particular reward to which it corresponds. In human terms, thinking in a particular way is only encouraged if the world behaves as we think it will: but actions can be learned for quite unconnected and arbitrary rewards. It is not justifiable therefore to apply the same terms and rules to internal and to external responses.

Another example is the experiment of Lawrence, on teaching a rat to pick out certain stimuli from a complex mass. The results not only require us to think of an internal response within the rat, but also make us suppose that learning such a response is harder than attaching an overt action to the internal response. If there were no such difference, the rat would not find it easier to learn new responses to the stimuli it had previously met. Once our attention is drawn to something, we readily notice changes in that thing which require different actions from us: but it is hard to notice something which has not previously aroused our attention. Thus here again there is a difference between external and internal responses, and it is not legitimate to apply the same rules to both.

As yet most behaviour theory does not seem to have found a satisfactory means of dealing with this difficulty and describing events within the brain in a fashion which marks them off from external actions. There are really two interconnected difficulties. One is the fact that any statement about unobservables can only be made by inference, and it is therefore necessary to be exceedingly cautious. This difficulty is unavoidable, and provides a very rational basis for the reluctance of most behaviour theorists to abandon the language of stimulus and response. But it is worth pointing out that the difficulties of inference are not avoided by saying that the unobservable is a very small twitch of a muscle rather than a burst of firing in the cortex.

The second difficulty is the quite distinct one of finding words for internal processes which can be understood without ambiguity. This snag does not lie in the nature of the problem, as the difficulty of inference does, and a solution may therefore be found for it. Some recent developments do suggest a line which may lead to a solution, and although it is far too early as yet to be confident that this is the line which behaviour theory will take, it is worth describing them.

## The Rise of Complex Mechanical Analogies

In the modern world there are numerous machines whose purpose is control or calculation. Unlike most earlier human devices, they do not primarily generate or transmit power, but rather manipulate events which symbolize facts in the external world. For example, an electronic computer may be fed with a paper tape punched with a series of holes. Each group of holes corresponds to a particular number, and, as the tape is fed in, a particular series of pulses which also corresponds to that number, may be generated in the computer. The series of pulses may be kept separate for a time, and then combined with another series so as to give a third series which corresponds to the sum of the two numbers represented by the original two series. This sum may then be stored by conversion into a pattern of magnetization on a drum, and finally be typed out with other figures by an automatic typewriter. At each stage in the process there is a physical event which corresponds to the number, although the event may be quite different from the number itself. A system of this sort, in which a set of alternative events correspond to a set of alternative inputs, so that any particular one of the latter gives rise to a particular one of the former, can be referred to as a system which handles 'information'. As we said in the first chapter, a whole branch of modern engineering is devoted to the study of the behaviour of such systems in the abstract, divorced from any particular physical method of representing each input. For example, if a given system contains only a limited number of alternative states, and can change between them at a particular speed, it can only deal with a certain numerical amount of information in a given time, no matter what the code adopted: and no matter whether the system is a telephone line, a radio frequency band, or some device of a quite different nature. Mathematical equations have been developed relating this maximum rate to the probability of the alternative signals and to similar factors: and these equations apply to any physical system for which their assumptions are true.

A particularly interesting group of systems are servo-mechanisms. Typically, these are devices which carry out some action but are provided with a sense-organ to detect the discrepancy between the result of that action and some desired situation. For instance, an automatic furnace may have an oil pump which feeds a certain quantity of fuel to the fire; and a thermometer which detects the temperature in the room. If the temperature is too high, the oil feed is reduced, and if it is too low the feed is increased. The advantage of such a system is, that it corrects for any unusual circumstances such as cold weather, a slight block in the oil-pipe reducing the fuel supply, or a particularly good brand of oil which gives more heat. If we draw a diagram to show the flow of information in a servo-mechanism there is a 'feed-back' path from the output to the input. By including this path the system is made more flexible and adaptible.*

Servo-mechanisms also can be analysed mathematically in the abstract, in a fashion rather different from the 'information theory' analysis of telephone lines and radio channels. In servo theory one seeks to predict the speed with which any disturbance will be corrected by the servo, the stability with which the output will

* A simple thermostat, in which output varies with the discrepancy from some desired output, should properly be called a regulator and not a servo-mechanism, because such a device will never quite cancel out the discrepancy. In a true servo the rate of change of output, and perhaps higher differentials, vary with the discrepancy and the latter can then be abolished in the steady state.

settle down after a disturbance, the presence of any 'resonant' frequency at which the output is exceptionally large for a given size of input, and so on.

Since computers can in a loose way be described as 'thinking' and since servo-mechanisms are apparently purposive, hunting for a goal which when attained brings inaction, it is not surprising that various attempts have been made to apply to biology analogies from these devices. Some of these attempts have been unsuccessful because they do not take into account the knowledge we already have about behaviour. As we have seen in earlier chapters, many of the first guesses, which are likely to occur to any intelligent person speculating about behaviour, have already occurred to psychologists and have been disproved. So the odds are heavily against any computer engineer who tries to set up a theory of behaviour without reference to the existing ones. Theories similar to those of Watson, and of Hull, have indeed been put forward in the new language: but the objections to them remain the same.

A second group of attempts have met with limited success. These are applications to behaviour of the mathematics of information theory and of servo theory, considering the nervous system as an unanalysable whole with no speculation about the flow of information within it. For instance, one can study the speed with which men react to signals of various probability and attempt to fit the results to the mathematical equations designed for single telephone or radio channels. Some success can be obtained in this way, and for particular types of signal and response it does seem that the assumptions of information theory do hold true for the human nervous system: but the value of the 'capacity', the maximum speed at which information can be handled, varies with the particular kind of signal and response. The validity of information theory used in this rather Skinnerian way is therefore much like that of Estes' theory mentioned earlier; it works within its limits but not outside them. This is not altogether surprising. Merely from the anatomy of the brain we would expect the

G 193

information from the senses to travel long paths which diverge and converge, which put some of the information into store, which feed-back from one part of the system to an earlier one, and which are at least as complicated as those of a man-made computer. It can only be under very special conditions that such a system can be treated as one simple straight-line channel from senses to muscles. The neglect of any possible internal complexities is an over-simplification of the same type as the traditional behaviourist treatment of observed and unobserved responses as identical.

Servo theory has similar difficulties. If we ask a man to control something, such as holding a flag steady in a gusty breeze, we can see that he does behave in typical servo fashion. He exerts a certain force, lessens it if he sees that he has pushed too hard, increases it when he sees that the wind is blowing stronger, and so on. It is possible to measure in human performance many of the same quantities which are measured for mechanical servos. Unfortunately it is quite clear that the mathematics usually used cannot legitimately be applied to the human case. They assume that, for instance, if the servo responds to an input A with an output $a$, and to an input B with an output $b$, that its response to $A + B$ will be $a + b$. This is not true of a human being, who changes in a bewildering fashion from being one kind of servo to being another, according to the situation in which he finds himself. In this case also, therefore, it is not good enough simply to treat the nervous system as a sealed black box and make no attempt to decide what its internal organization is. Without some assumption on that point, no regularity can be obtained in the observed behaviour.

The methods of measurement derived from engineering systems do not therefore change the conclusion which we drew from experiments conceived in the older language of stimulus and response. Laws which are simply statements of observed behaviour will only hold in particular restricted situations. If we want to be more ambitious and to give a scientific account of the changes between one situation and another, we have to introduce theoretical concepts going beyond observation. Now another possible use of mechanical analogies is to do this: to provide a language for discussing events within the animal's head without using ambiguous words derived from human experience. The definition of a feed-back path ought to create less uncertainty than that of 'mixed feelings', and correspondingly we should be able to decide more readily whether there is evidence for such paths or not.

The difficulty is still likely to remain, however, that the pattern of events within the head has to be inferred from outside. The easiest way of showing how this can be done is to take some examples, which may indeed prove to be mistaken when more evidence has accumulated, but which happen to be familiar to the present writer and which show how argument can proceed from the outside to the inside of the nervous system.

In the first place, Deutsch has put forward a model for the learning process which is based on servo analogies. Leaving his specialized terminology aside, the essence of his theory is that a network is built up inside the brain, the parts of the net being related to one another in the same way as the parts of the outer world are to one another. Thus if a rat has repeatedly experienced a pathway from place A to place C via place B, there are three corresponding parts of the nervous system which are linked in the order A B C. If a drive is present, the network is activated at those points which represent the events concerned with satisfying the drive. So if food has been present at place C, the hungry rat will have his network activated from the point corresponding to C. The activity spreads to the parts of the net furthest away from the point at which it enters; and at the furthest point it brings into action a servo-system which is so designed that it will vary the actions of the animal until the senses are stimulated by the event corresponding to that part of the net. Thus, in our rat example, the animal will vary its actions until it finds itself at place A, the start of the pathway. When it is at A, the relevant servo is switched off and the next nearest to C (the source of the activation of the network) comes into action. This, in the example, will cause the animal to proceed to B, and so on to C. The conception is rather like that of a succession of devices resembling the automatic furnace we mentioned earlier.

Suppose for instance that our furnace was linked to other devices, so that as soon as the room temperature had been brought to a desired level the heat was next applied to bath-water; and, when that had reached a certain level, the oil was fed to a burner heating a kettle. Finally when the kettle reached boiling point the oil was switched off and an alarm sounded to waken the person whose room, bath, and tea had been prepared. Such a train of mechanisms is basically understandable enough: and Deutsch suggests that a rat running a maze is acting as a similar group of connected feed-back devices.

Some of the evidence for this theory has already been mentioned in other connections. For instance, once a rat has walked through a maze he will still be able to find his way through even if we fill the maze with water and make him swim through. The action taken by the servo need not be the same on each occasion, so long as it produces the correct result: our temperature regulator may have to increase the oil flow on some days and decrease it on others, depending on the weather, but it always reaches the same temperature in the end. Deutsch's theory explains therefore the curious variability of the actions which an animal or a man may take on different occasions to attain the same end. This variability is difficult to account for if we think in terms of the learning of particular responses. As the point is an important one, it is worth giving a last example of it. Suppose we get a man to rest his hand, palm down, on an electric contact; and give him a shock every time we ring a bell. We will soon develop a strong conditioned response to the bell, so that he will bend his hand back at the wrist and lift it off the contact. If now we turn his hand over, back down, and ring the bell we do not find that the same muscles contract and so press the hand firmly against the source of the shock. On the contrary the opposite muscles operate, bend the hand forward at the wrist, and secure the same end of lifting the hand away from the shock. There is no problem here if we think of the process of learning as the creation of a feed-back loop such that it will secure a separation between hand and contact: but the experiment is baffling if we think in terms of the attachment of responses to stimuli.

A second merit of Deutsch's theory is that it harmonizes readily with experimental results on reward and motive, discussed in the last chapter. The goal sought by an animal will be the stimulation closest to the satisfaction of its needs at that time, and it will seek even stimuli which do not themselves satisfy the need – such as the sight of a female or the taste of saccharin. All the evidence showing that reward consists in the arrival of certain stimuli, rather than in the satisfaction of a physical need, is therefore consistent with Deutsch's succession of linked servo-mechanisms.

One last example, previously mentioned in another connection, can serve as an illustration of the experiments which Deutsch's theory suggests and to which it is likely to give rise in the future. Suppose we take a hungry rat and put it in a T-maze with food in both arms of the maze. In one arm only we put water. Then we make the rat thirsty and put it back in the maze. Will it go straight to the water, or did it ignore the water as long as it was hungry? To some extent the animal does show knowledge of the position of the water, but its performance depends very much on the exact arrangement of the experiment. For instance, it makes a difference whether the water was just by the junction of the T-maze, or whether it was close by the food. Now on the Law of Effect, all responses (internal or external) made just before food was reached should be better learned than those made earlier in the maze. Therefore the rat ought to do better when the water was near the food. On Deutsch's theory, on the other hand, activation spreading inside the rat's brain through the net which symbolizes the maze, will spread differently in the two cases. Since there is food in both alleys, they are similar in that respect and their symbolic representations inside the rat will be joined at the point corresponding to food. If then the water is near the food, activation from it will spread almost equally through the parts corresponding to both alleys: while if the water is far from the food the activation will be much stronger in the correct alley than in the wrong one, because it has further to go to leap across to the incorrect one. So on Deutsch's theory the rat ought to do better when the water is well away from the food. In fact it does, and the experiment therefore supports his interpretation rather than a Hullian one in terms of $r_g$s occurring internally.

The use of a theory of the events inside the brain, expressed in terms derived from a mechanical analogy, has to be hypothetico-deductive. That is, there have to be guesses followed by experimental checks. But it is possible to be cautious in the guessing, and to consider what the possible alternative theories are, so as to avoid the dangers discussed in Chapter V. Thus one can contrast a closed-loop system like Deutsch's with an open-chain one like Hull's containing no feed-back path: broadly speaking the brain must fall into one category or the other, and from its behaviour we can decide which. As we have seen, the evidence seems to incline towards the servo analogy, although no doubt Deutsch's theory will require further modification in the years to come.

Our second example comes from the use of information theory rather than servo-theory. We mentioned earlier that the amount of information which could be transmitted through any physical system in a given time was limited. Now this is presumably true of the nervous system as well: and a number of experiments have shown that men cannot react efficiently to large numbers of unpredictable signals all arriving simultaneously. In ordinary language, they are distracted by one stimulus so that they cannot deal efficiently with another. While you are reading this, you are probably not aware of the pressure of your chair against your body: unless your attention wanders for a moment. It has therefore been suggested that the incoming information from the senses is filtered and only part of it passes through the brain to produce learning or action. Most of the experiments performed to support this view are conducted on human beings, but there are analogies in animal behaviour which have allowed the theory to be applied

to other species. For instance, in man there is evidence that prolonged work requiring attention to one class of stimuli produces
occasional failure to notice such stimuli: which is interpreted by
the theory as being due to a shift of the filter away from that type
of information to some other type. The experiments on animals
exploring novel objects and failing to react to familiar ones, cited
in the last chapter, can be regarded as analogous to the human
behaviour and as evidence for a similar filtering of information as
it enters an animal's brain. The process of inference, by which the
existence of a filter in animals is deduced, can be illustrated by an
experiment of Pavlov's. Suppose you try and condition a dog to
salivate when you apply gentle heat to his body. This can be done
easily enough. So also can he be taught to salivate when you
touch him, and of course if you do both together. But now suppose that one trains an animal from the beginning with heat and
touch together, and he has never met either separately. Once he is
trained, he will react to the touch alone: but not to the heat alone.
No learning has taken place of the connection between heat and
food. This cannot be because the heat is too faint a stimulus (it
produced learning when given alone). Nor is it because of any
difficulty in the response. It must be that one stimulus (touch)
somehow prevented the other (heat) from taking any effect upon
the part of the nervous system where learning takes place. The
information was in other words filtered, and the heat did not get
through the filter.

The process of argument in this case is not based on the guess-
and-check method but upon deductions from observation. While
this is the ideal way of drawing an information flow diagram for
the nervous system, there are probably limits to the extent to
which it is possible. Certainly the suggestion that filtering takes
place in other situations is a guess, but one supported by a certain
amount of evidence. Lawrence's experiment on teaching rats to
notice certain stimuli will be remembered. One important suggestion is that, while any information which passes the filter is
likely to be learned quite independent of reward, yet an animal in

a drive-state is more likely to notice matters connected with reward. Such a view would reconcile the undoubted tendency for reward to produce more visible learning, and the awkward cases in which learning takes place without reward. As we saw in the last chapter, an animal whose basic needs are satisfied is more likely than an animal who is very hungry or thirsty to learn things without being rewarded for it. But far more evidence is needed on this topic, since it is generally agreed that reward is needed to secure performance even if an unproductive learning may take place without it. A lazy man may learn how to do a job although nobody rewards him for learning, and yet fail to do it unless it is made worth his while. This fact alone may account for the greater ease with which learning can be demonstrated when reward is present: it is not certain that any other theoretical factor is required.

The idea, that information entering the nervous system is filtered and not all produces an effect, is one which is closely linked with the present writer himself and may therefore have obtained too much prominence. But this theory like Deutsch's suggests that the next step in the analysis of behaviour is the construction of theories about the events within the skull. Whether cybernetic analogies ultimately provide the agreed language for this step, or whether a purified description in terms of $r_g$s proves adequate, this is the topic to which psychologists are turning.

## The Endless Search

We end then upon a note of doubt, with no certainty about the beliefs which future psychologists will hold. This is as it should be. Nobody can grasp the nature of things from an armchair, and until fresh experiments have been performed we do not know what their results will be. The confident dogmatisms about human nature which fall so readily from pulpits, newspaper editorials, and school prize-givings are not for us. Rather we must be prepared to live with an incomplete knowledge of behaviour but with confidence in the power of objective methods to give us that knowledge some day. Those methods have proved themselves even in the past fifty years. Looking back we can see them destroying one over-simplification after another, forcing us to reject Pavlov's theory or Hull's and bringing theoretical opponents closer together by the sheer weight of factual evidence. In this half-century there has been recognizable progress in our understanding of behaviour, typified by the plan of this book. We have gone from the crude ideas of Watsonian conditioning, through the plain Law of Effect, to the more sophisticated ideas of acquired drives (anxiety) and $r_g$s; and from those to the importance of learning in producing mechanisms which allow more complex perception and insight, and to the biological importance of exploration. As now we turn to our mathematical models and mechanical analogies, there is no question that we are further on than Watson was: and that a true gain in knowledge has taken place. For fifty years, the gain is not so bad. It is very doubtful whether the difference between the nineteenth century and classical antiquity was, in this field of knowledge, as great as that in the time we have covered.

Nevertheless, we are still only scratching the surface. The discrepancy, between our partial success at saying which of two paths a rat will choose and the human problems which surround us, is appalling. It is hardly surprising therefore if some people grow impatient with this laborious laying of brick upon brick, and long for quicker results. To this longing there are two answers. On the one hand, the uncertainty of our present knowledge need not stop us from acting in practical situations, making for the purpose the best guess we can. By all means therefore let us listen to the intuitive insights of saints, psychiatrists, and even politicians, into human nature: listen, and choose what seems best. But on the other hand, let us never forget that our choice may be wrong, and the methods we use to bring up children or reform criminals *may* be having exactly the wrong result if we have not tested them objectively. If a technique of curing neurosis is valid, it ought to meet the same criteria as a method of curing tuberculosis does:

that is, more people should get better amongst those subjected to the cure than amongst those having some different kind of treatment. If we become so convinced of our intuitive method that we neglect to support it by evidence, we may be doing positive harm. There is more than a suspicion that some methods of treating neurotics do no good at all, but go on simply because nobody has ever put them to an objective test: is this really an improvement on the slow step-by-step method of scientific advance, or is it rather a hindrance to progress?

There are therefore great dangers in any attempt to short-cut the study of behaviour. From all the labours of the past fifty years, three main lessons can perhaps be learned for everyday life: and the first of these is that an objective attitude to behaviour is possible and essential if we are not to accept glib generalizations. When, for example, we are told that income-tax discourages the working of overtime in industry, our response should not be to ask ourselves if this is intuitively reasonable, but to see whether the records of an actual factory support the statement.* When we put the knobs on a gas-stove we should not put them in the place which seems natural to us, but try out a number of arrangements on a large sample of the people who might use the stove. In many of the cases in which we blandly make assumptions about human nature, it is possible to get evidence. Although we may lack a sweeping general theory of behaviour, we can lean much more heavily on objective evidence in detached matters than most of us do.

The second broad lesson is that behaviour whose roots are simple and determinate has nevertheless issued, even in the rat, into something much more complex and self-regulating. The necessity to cope rapidly with changing circumstances has led by stages to foresight and choice, if (as seems reasonable) those terms can be applied to the internal trial of anticipatory responses and the execution of the most desired action. At this stage and still more in ourselves it is possible for the brain to determine its own

* In the only research on this subject known to the author they do not.

future rather than producing stereotyped actions laid down by heredity or stamped in by environment. Both factors play their part in building up the mechanism, but the actions of a rat are not laid down in detail in its genes nor are they simply repetitions of past actions which have been rewarded. We can see already how the mechanism of decision can be disordered – by a failure of childhood experience, or by an anxiety so great attached to certain acts that they are never even thought of – but when the mechanism is operating it is responsible for its own actions. There is no warrant for treating human beings as bundles of isolated responses, when greater levels of organization and complexity are found in animals less elaborate than ourselves.

This brings us to the third main lesson of behaviour theory. The complexity which appears in the rat and even more in ourselves is flexible rather than rigid. Our extraordinary talents are for learning, not for performing some rigid pattern of behaviour. No matter how ingrained our feeling that *this* is the natural way to behave, there is usually little warrant for it. Our society and we ourselves could behave in a quite different fashion, although a change may be hard to produce now that we have grown old. We could have regarded the relation between man and wife as one of natural competition and hostility; other societies do. We could have been co-operative and self-effacing; people in other societies are. The style of conduct which we should adopt is variable over wide ranges, even though limits will be set by features of behaviour already mentioned such as the need for reward. Any choice we make will be arbitrary, even that of acquiescing in the particular conventions of our surroundings. Although it is common to regard this latter choice as 'natural' it is not so. It is just as natural to reject the mode of life which we and all of our neighbours live, and to direct our efforts towards some other.

Each of us has to make this choice for himself, since there can be no agreed rule for making it. It is a choice like that between the metric system and English units of measure: it is not like a choice between different numbers as representing the mileage from A to B. The reader has probably made his own choice: to many people, even the best things in our own society and in all others upon this planet seem in need of change. Different men have different reasons for coming to this view, and obtain their vision of the future from a variety of sources. For the writer, the standard of reference is a Christian one.

Against the perspective of two thousand years the speed of our advance in studying human nature seems more cheerful. At a rough guess, two hundred more years may bring the study of behaviour up to the level which physics reached in Newton's time. The problem to be faced is less tractable than that of the organization of the Solar System, but it is for that very reason of overwhelming scientific interest. It is in this field rather than the study of simpler systems that the great triumphs of scientific method will come: not in the life-time of those who become psychologists today, but amongst those who make use of their results tomorrow. For many of us, even though we shall probably not see that triumph, the most exciting frontier of knowledge is far closer than the borders of space. It walks beside us in the street.

# Appendix
## on the Explanation of Insight

The explanation of insightful behaviour in Hullian terms, given in Chapter IV, is different from that current in much of the literature. The reason is that Hull's theory provides several ways in which this behaviour might be explained, and I thought it best to keep to that used originally by Hull himself (*Psychological Review*, 1935, **42**, 219–45). This explanation is essentially one in terms of internal trial-and-error, since it does not regard $r_g$ as elicited directly by any external stimulus present at the time of decision, but rather considers the crucial mediation to take place through another fractional response. If the rat is combining two previously learned segments of behaviour, AB and BG, one of which starts from the animal's present position A, and the other of which ends with reward G, the fractional response corresponding to B (the end of one segment and the beginning of the other) must occur. This in turn might then give rise to $r_g$ through the stimulation produced by $r_B$, but the latter is essential. Thus success may not be achieved until the correct fractional response is tried and the process is true internal trial-and-error.

But one might also suppose that, if the animal learns BG first, $r_g$ becomes attached to the stimuli at B. In that case, when AB is being learned $r_g$ will occur as soon as B is reached. Since $r_g$ will then be reinforced by whatever reward is used to teach AB, $r_g$ will occur simply to A, although this will not affect behaviour until the animal is appropriately motivated. When, however, a drive is present which would be satisfied by the reward which $r_g$ represents, A will produce $r_g$ and so the sequence of action ABG.

In this case no internal response other than $r_g$ occurs and thus this explanation is not really one in terms of internal trial-and-error.

C. E. Osgood, in his widely used text *Method and Theory in Experimental Psychology*, gives this simpler explanation and points out that it predicts that the rat could not learn to combine AB and BG if it learned AB first. Hull's original explanation is not restricted in this way, and it will be remembered that the Tolman-Miller controversy provides a case in which AB was learned first but successful performance resulted. Furthermore the simpler theory runs into the difficulty that $r_g$ has to be strengthened by a reward other than that which produces the full response of which $r_g$ is a component. As we have seen, Deutsch has effectively criticized any theory which requires this to happen. I have therefore set out the theory of internal trial-and-error rather than the simpler version but the latter is certainly a legitimate deduction from Hull's postulates even though it is not the one which he himself put forward in the first place.

There are two other similar points. The first concerns the extent to which the occurrence of $r_g$ at the beginning of a learned sequence of actions, depends upon a chain of fractional responses corresponding to the sequence of actions. I have described it as so doing, when it would also be possible for $r_g$ to be directly conditioned to the first stimulus of the sequence, provided the after-effects of that stimulus were still reverberating in the nervous system at the time when reward was given. This kind of mechanism would not require so detailed a symbolic model in the nervous system, but would be subject to the limitation that reward must occur rapidly after the first stimulus in the sequence. I have therefore given the more general theory as less likely to be disproved in the future, and as equally deducible from Hull's theory.

The second point concerns the mechanism by which $r_g$ initiates overt action. One possible suggestion is that, since at an early stage of learning $r_g$ becomes attached to the first stimuli in the learned sequence, $r_g$ is occurring when later actions are made. Thus the self-produced stimulation arising from $r_g$ becomes conditioned to these actions, and thus $r_g$ gives a greater tendency to action. Such an explanation is plausible and parsimonious, but there is no direct evidence for it, and it seems to be unable to explain insightful behaviour except by the restricted theory already mentioned in this Appendix. A theory of internal trial-and-error would not suppose $r_g$ to be present during the learning of AB (to revert to our example), and therefore $r_g$ could not assist performance by providing extra stimuli tending to elicit action. In this case also I have therefore adhered to Hull's early papers rather than to later commentators.

# Suggestions for Further Reading

*Chapter 1*

For the history of psychology at the period in question:

E. G. BORING. *A History of Experimental Psychology*. Appleton Century 1933

E. R. HILGARD and D. G. MARQUIS. *Conditioning and Learning*. Appleton Century 1940

For an account of heredity and environment in their effects on intelligence:

J. M. BLACKBURN. *The Framework of Human Behaviour*. Routledge 1947

For the effect of society in moulding individual personality:

MARGARET MEAD. *Sex and Temperament in Three Primitive Societies*. Mentor 1950

For Watson's own views:

J. B. WATSON. *Behaviourism*. University of Chicago Press 1924.

For more sophisticated defences of behaviourism:

K. S. LASHLEY. *Psychological Review*, 1923, **30,** 237–72, 329–53

E. C. TOLMAN. *Psychological Review*, 1922, **29,** 44–53. (Reprinted in *Behavior and Psychological Man*, University of California Press 1958)

*Chapter 2*

For accounts of animal behaviour:

N. TINBERGEN. *The Study of Instinct*. Oxford University Press 1951.

W. H. THORPE. *Learning and Instinct in Animals*. Methuen 1956.

For evolution:

J. M. SMITH. *The Theory of Evolution*. Penguin Books 1958.

For the Law of Effect and its difficulties:

E. R. HILGARD. *Theories of Learning.* (First edition 1948.) (Second edition 1956.) Appleton Century. (The first edition gives Hull's earlier views and the second his later ones, so that both are worth examining)

For the latest version of Hullian theory:

K. W. SPENCE. *Behaviour Theory and Conditioning.* Yale University Press 1956


*Chapter 3*

For reviews of acquired drives and of conflict between motives:

N. E. MILLER, in S. S. Stevens, ed, *Handbook of Experimental Psychology.* Wiley 1951

N. E. MILLER, in J. Mc V. Hunt, ed, *Personality and the Behavior Disorders.* Ronald 1944.

For Mowrer's views at various times:

O. H. MOWRER. *Learning Theory and Personality Dynamics.* Ronald 1950

For the differential effects of alcohol on approach and avoidance:

J. J. CONGER. *Quarterly Journal of Studies on Alcohol,* 1951, **12,** 1–29

For experimental neurosis:

J. H. MASSERMAN. *Behavior and Neurosis.* University of Chicago Press 1943

For the development of ulcers in animals kept under approach-avoidance conflict:

W. L. SAWREY and J. D. WEISZ. *Journal of Comparative and Physiological Psychology,* 1956, **49,** 269–70


*Chapter 4*

For the Tolman–Miller controversy:

E. C. TOLMAN. *Psychological Review,* 1933, **40,** 246–55

N. E. MILLER. *Psychological Review,* 1935, **42,** 280–92

For Köhler's classic work on apes:

W. KÖHLER. *The Mentality of Apes*. Harcourt Brace 1925

For a recent view of Tolman's experiment on insight in rats:

W. S. ANTHONY. *British Journal of Psychology*, 1959, **50**, 117–24

For the reasoning experiments and their explanation:

N. R. F. MAIER. *Comparative Psychology Monographs*, No. 29, 1929.

C. L. HULL. *Psychological Review*, 1935, **42**, 219–45

For recent views on the fractional anticipatory response:

J. A. DEUTSCH. *Psychological Review*, 1956, **63**, 389–99

B. F. RITCHIE. *British Journal of Psychology*, 1959, **50**, 1–15

For the experiment on varying the relation between goal-box colour and reward and its significance:

L. B. WYCKOFF. *Psychological Review*, 1959, **66**, 68–78

Chapter 5

For the approach of Hull, and the prediction concerning rise in recall with delay after learning:

C. L. HULL. *Psychological Review*, 1935, **42**, 491–516.

For the approach of Skinner:

B. F. SKINNER. *The Behavior of Organisms*. Appleton Century 1938

B. F. SKINNER. *Psychological Review*, 1950, **57**, 193–216

B. F. SKINNER. *Verbal Behavior*. Methuen 1959

For the effect of reinforcement on human beings, as in the increase of statements of opinion:

L. KRASNER. *Psychological Bulletin*, 1958, **55**, 148–170

For methodological criticism of Hull:

S. KOCH in ESTES, KOCH, MACCORQUODALE, MEEHL, MUELLER, SCHOENFELD, and VERPLANCK. *Modern Learning Theory*, Appleton Century 1954.

Chapter 6

For Lashley's early experiments:

K. S. LASHLEY. *Brain Mechanisms and Intelligence*. Chicago University Press 1929

C. T. MORGAN in S. S. Stevens, ed, *Handbook of Experimental Psychology*
Wiley 1951

For the importance of pattern in perception:

M. D. VERNON. *A Further Study of Visual Perception.* Cambridge University Press 1952

For Hebb's theory:

D. O. HEBB. *The Organisation of Behavior.* Wiley 1949

For the effect of conductors placed across the brain:

K. S. LASHLEY, K. L. CHOW, and JOSEPHINE SEMMES. *Psychological Review*, 1951, **58**, 123–36

For the effect of familiarity with shapes in allowing rats to learn to discriminate them:

E. J. GIBSON and R. D. WALK. *Journal of Comparative and Physiological Psychology*, 1956, **49**, 239–42

For the advantage of reversing a relationship as opposed to learning an entirely fresh one:

M. HARROW and G. R. FRIEDMAN. *Journal of Experimental Psychology*, 1958, **55**, 592–8

D. H. LAWRENCE. *Journal of Experimental Psychology*, 1950, **40**, 175–88

For the disabilities of children deprived early in life:

J. BOWLBY. *Maternal Care and Mental Health.* World Health Organization 1952

For the ability to learn to wear distorting spectacles:

J. G. TAYLOR and S. PAPERT. *British Journal of Psychology*, 1956, 47, 216–224

For the effect of stimulating a 'reward' centre in the brain:

J. OLDS and P. MILNER. *Journal of Comparative & Physiological Psychology.* 1954, 47, 419–27

*Chapter 7*

For reviews of the experiments on exploration and alternation:

M. GLANZER. *Psychological Bulletin*, 1958, **55**, 302–315

S. A. BARNETT. *British Journal of Psychology*, 1958, **49**, 289–310

For the experiment on kittens:

R. C. MILES. *Journal of Comparative & Physiological Psychology.* 1958, **51**, 39–42


Chapter 8

For the mathematical theories of learning:

E. R. HILGARD. *Theories of Learning* (2nd Ed. 1956). Appleton Century

For experiments showing that guessing-game behaviour varies with instructions and the gains or losses possible:

J. J. GOODNOW. *American Journal of Psychology*, 1955, **68**, 106–16

E. H. GALANTER and W. A. SMITH. *American Journal of Psychology*, 1958, **71**, 359–66

For theories in terms of information-flow:

D. E. BROADBENT. *Perception and Communication.* Pergamon 1958

# Index

# University Paperbacks

## A COMPLETE LIST OF TITLES

Titles marked thus: * are to be published during 1966

## ARCHAEOLOGY AND ANTHROPOLOGY

## ART AND ARCHITECTURE

## BIOGRAPHY

## ECONOMICS

# LAW

# LITERATURE